Silence is Violence

#Me Too/Military Sexual Trauma (MST)

By

Heidi Lobstein MSN, RN

Rank

I'm sitting on a wooden bench contemplating my position. The grass stripes the earth beneath my feet. I see individual blades fresh and vibrant green. I see patches where clusters of crab grass form taller than the other blades. The grass covers the soil and keeps the dirt in place. Behind me is the back of the bench. It's sturdy and gives me support. Beyond the bench is a silver ladder leaning against the trunk of a huge big tree. The ladder reaches upward toward the golden silver leaves. With feathers shining in the brightness of the sun, an eagle swoops down among the branches. The full bird soon takes flight again, flapping its wings. It sores upward toward the one star and is soon out of site. I'm sitting on a wooden bench contemplating my position.

Nurse Interns 1987

Heidi Lolotein 2LT

6

Preface

My sister Heidi evolved into an empathic wounded healer during the 30 years of mystery between her gang rapes and the VA system's relatively new Military Sexual Trauma or MST program. Our family was clueless about her trauma until the MST program at the VA unraveled the cause of her 30 years of repression and PTSD acting out and apparent need for psychiatric prescription. I am happy to witness first-hand her unfoldment and release of the repression with her Cognitive Processing Therapy.

Before her MST, Heidi was normally thin as the reader can

see pictures of in this book. The long-term use of psychiatric meds such as Depakote and Risperidone caused physical damage. Depakote is supposed to be for epilepsy which she never had, toxified and damaged her liver, gave her fatty liver, and caused her to gain massive weight. Risperidone is indicated for the short-term treatment of bipolar disorder, but was prescribed long-term. Psychiatrists who were dealing in the dark with PTSD of unknown etiology, as Heidi and the family and the psychiatrists were not consciously aware of her MST history, prescribed petrochemical pharmaceutical medications. As a health scientist, exercise physiologist,

and metaphysician of Asian
medicine, I was able to help
wean her off about 17 meds and
we honed it down to two with
better nutrition and exercise
and some weight loss, and we
got her to drain the Damp or
fluid retention causing edema or
puffy skin. Although she had
been in therapy and hypnosis
for general anxiety and stress
for decades, this recovery was
mostly accelerated by Heidi's
discovery of the apparently
well-hidden MST program at the
West LA VA led by Dr.
Himmelfarb. This program is
relatively new and not well
marketed to our understanding,
having started as recently as
2007, but discovered by Heidi in
2012.

Unfortunately until about 2007 and until this day, the military and VA system remains negligent in dealing with rape trauma and its PTSD consequences, especially since 25% of all women military personnel are raped and therefore compromised with MST caused PTSD. We found that after 30 years, nothing much has changed in bureaucratic attitudes towards military warriors who were wounded in this way. This must change and the military and or the VA must have a coordinated effort to deal with this, rather than continuing to pretend the problem doesn't exist. For example, had the VA Employee

Health Doctor been aware that Cognitive Processing Therapy (CPT) causes labile emotions to surface during the course of therapy for PTSD from MST, he would have understood why Heidi could not process his memo or letter of April 2017 directing her to be evaluated by her own doctors. This knowledge would have avoided the questionable validity, reliability, and objectivity of testing her, which was designed for screening cadet entry into the police academy, that probably erroneously concluded she is "unfit for duty." The psychometric tests may have been used inappropriately, and the continued withholding of Heidi's record file from the psychological evaluation suggests this may be the case. To this date, Heidi has not received a copy of this test file with written interpretations of the data – although she requested it on numerous occasions. I observe information about the test validity with experience in using psychometric testing in my research reported in peer-reviewed psychiatric and scientific journals, and from my teaching graduate courses for decades in tests and measurement, including psychometric testing, and research design and statistics.

The entire VA system needs to have a director of MST therapy so that education of military personnel can be coordinated with marketing, recognized consequences of rape, and treatment of rape survivor veterans. The conduct of the VA Employee Health Doctor, at the time Heidi was railroaded out of the VA system after being a competent psych nurse for 30 years, illustrates that VA employee education about MST matters is desperately and sorely needed.

Dennis Lobstein, MTCM, PhD
Doctor of Health and Exercise Science and Master of Asian Medicine

14

Coming to Planet Earth

My Birth

I was delivered by
Cesarean section. Placenta-
Previa. My placenta was
coming out into this world
before me.... not a good
thing. I was told I was all
kinds of funny colors...blue,
yellow, green. Since I was a

teenager I would call my
Mom up on my birthday
and wish her a Happy Labor
and delivery day. She would
say, "But dear...you were
Cesarean!!!" The fact is she
still went through labor
pains until the emergency
C-section. Furthermore,
they cut her vertically
causing her abdominal
muscles to heal resulting in
two aprons of flesh hanging
from her abdomen, which
was common with
Cesareans back in those
days. Oh yes, she let me
know how I had caused this
unpleasant change to her
body! I learned early on
how I was to be responsible
for my mother's wellbeing.

I heard my dad was very proud of having a girl, and he carried me like a football around the nursery. I was also told that I cried for 3 or 4 bottles of milk when most babies were satisfied with one. I'm an Aries...March 22, 1963 around 10AM. Aries are known for their voracious appetites!

I am the third child and a girl born into a Jewish family with a history. I have two older brothers, and they were born vaginally. All three of us were born out in California at Cedars of Lebanon in Los Angeles. We moved across country to Lafayette, Indiana when I was two years old. The trip across country was a lesson in object

permanence for me. I
remembered I left my tiny tears
baby doll in the restaurant about
150miles later and my dad
would not go back to get it!
I was very difficult to console as
by then I had the concept that
the doll was sitting all alone
back in the restaurant. I was a
bad mommy abandoning her
dolly leaving it to the mercy of
strangers! My brothers were
both amused by my distress. I
was still in diapers on this trip.
My mom became so distracted
by my brother's shtick jumping
up and down on the hotel bed
singing "Happy Davis" that she
put Crest toothpaste on my
diaper rash instead of Desitin!
When I reacted, fussing and

screaming my brothers went
into hysterics!

Then when we reached
Indiana my brother Harold,

seven years older than me, named the long rows of corn looking like legs running alongside the car "Jack."   Jack wore green pants but in new fields he changed to brown pants. He had the incredible ability to jump over houses and towns into the next field. When we got to a Motel in Lafayette, Indiana, Harold named the place Blue Bell's House after the maid that cleaned our room. His favorite activity was chasing me up and down the hallways to make me scream in joyous terror.

My Grandmothers

My two grandmothers were very different. My Grandmother on my father's side had nicknames for my brothers. Darwin who was 10 years older than me was Mr. Turkey and Harold was Mr. Carrot. I was just "The Gherrl." I guess that was a projection. Thirteen years later, on my Bat Mitzvah, my grandmother stood next to me in the reception line shaking hands with the congregation and said to me, "Yesterday I was nobody...today I am somebody." I told her, "You are always somebody, **you** are my Grandmother!" I don't think she liked that...She had a thing about aging. If you ask me, I would say that a successful life is just to become an interesting old person, and shouldn't be dependent on your grandchild's status. She liked to be called Muti, which means mother in German. She survived the Holocaust. Being a beautiful woman she could work her magic on an Austrian officer who had been in WWI fighting against the Russians with my Grandfather who we called Fati meaning father in German. He could recognize Fati as a fellow officer. My grandmother, Muti could get my Grandfather, Fati out of a Vichy, France prison before as he in his typhoid condition got transferred to a concentration camp like Auschwitz. They came to New

York and then Chicago and eventually moved to California. Muti loved to swim. I inherited that aquatic ability. It kept her in good shape. She had been through trauma. Although disappointed, I understood why when I was only thirteen her Bat Mitzvah gift to me was a broken handled orange purse with smudges on it from a thrift store.

My grandma on my mother's side took care of me after the C-section. My mom was pretty wiped out with post-partum depression. My mom's mom was called Grandma. She was very giving...taking care of everyone but herself. She died of a stroke when I was six years old. She came to America to visit friends during the Cossack invasions in Russia when she was only sixteen. She couldn't go back because the village in Minsk, Russia where she was from had been destroyed. She made me a cloth pussycat...the lines from the pattern showing on it. She was having mini strokes at the time. I can see her arm coming out from behind the couch going to and fro as she sewed the pussycat. She lived with us in my early childhood. She used to be a practical nurse. She would take care of the whole family after the birth of a child. Cooking...cleaning...everything the mother who gave birth couldn't do after the delivery. I took after her. I am a nurse. I've been taking care of others even in childhood. My dad was very sick and I came into his room when I was about four bringing my blocks with me and spraying my magic healing spray emanating in my imagination from the blocks. I learned very young to take care of others needs first.

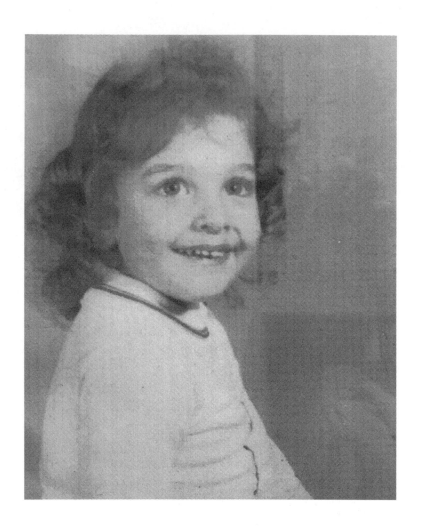

My Mother

I bonded very strongly with
my mother and had major

separation anxiety from my mother. I remember nursery school when my mom took me I hung onto the doorknob after she left and I cried the whole time. On the other hand, when my dad took me I went and played with the other kids! I even became enmeshed in my other relationships. In second grade I had a boyfriend named Gerald Handy. When the teacher moved our desks apart because we talked too much I had a complete hysterical meltdown. I remember the teacher, Miss Tarrell, telling me that we could still see each other from across the room. It was still too much for me to bear.

My whole family discussed and named me Heidi after the

movie with Shirley Temple. I'm glad they didn't name me Shirley!!! I certainly have the curls. My mom signed me up for tap dancing lessons at the YMCA. I did ok until my mom saw I was involved and decided to go to the store and shop across the street from the Y. As soon as I noticed my mom wasn't in the room watching me I ceased to function. I cried and wailed until she came back. So much for being an entertainer! My brothers loved my curls. I use to do "muff duffs" rotating my head rapidly back and forth causing a tirade of curls to go swinging and wildly cascading in all directions. I liked the back and forth motion. I have a vague memory of rocking my wheeled crib as I was up on my hands and knees rocking back and forth across the entire room!!!

My Father

Quite honestly my father scared me when I was a small child. He also survived the Holocaust at age fifteen by being sent to England after his older brother and ending up in an internment camp accused of being a German spy. He was lucky not to have the J for Jew stamped in his passport?! I know he was in some boarding house going to school in England and the woman in charge of the young men sexually molested him. There were boundary issues my dad had. When I was a teenager and in the bathroom after a shower he was in silly mode and made googly, eyes trying to look at me behind the towel I held in front of me using the mirror on the wall next to me. I was weirded out. Sometimes when he kissed me he would be acting silly and thrust his tongue past my lips. That grossed me out. I didn't like that. My mom was worried he would be inappropriate with me. When I was eleven and kissing my dad good night she yelled at me. "DON'T EVER BE KISSING YOUR FATHER GOOD NIGHT IN A DARKENED BEDROOM!" I felt like I had done something wrong. He also flew into angry rages and you learned very quickly to get out of his way. Every Sunday my mom would make a nice brunch. We would have Lox Bagel and Cream Cheese or Matzo Brie. Then after a nice Sunday brunch for no apparent reason my dad would get into a head rubbing mood…. frustrated and angry and stroking the top of his bald head. He would yell and swing out trying to hit us. My brothers and I learned to flee the area. I remember my oldest brother shoved me into the closet under the stairs to keep me safe. I heard yelling and screaming outside and didn't dare come out.

After a scene like that my dad would leave for a while. When he came back he would be happy and silly. "I'm

happy…let's all be happy now!"
My mom would pack up old
breadcrumbs for us to take to
Columbia Park to go feed the
ducks. My mom would sing:
QUACK A DACK A DACK
HERE COMES HEIDI WITH A
SNACK!!!
My dad and I were sent out to
play and get some fresh air. I felt
anxious like the other shoe was
going to drop but we had fun
anyway. My dad and I after
feeding the ducks would go on
the outside stage at Columbian
Park and "act" and "sing" and
"dance" …. We put on quite a
performance for the non-
existent crowd. We were
famous!!!! My dad could be very
silly.

The closet under the stairs
that I use to hide in for safety I
would also hide in to surprise
my dad when he came home
from work! It was the world of
the vacuum cleaner and
overcoats. I could wait in there a
long time. I imagined a secret

world in back of the closet were monsters lurked. I wouldn't go too far back for fear of being pulled into their world. I'd hang out in the safety of the overcoats. I was an imaginative kid who went to the market with my parents with a pot on my head and rubber boots on because that day I was an astronaut!

My dad and I went to Indian Princesses together too. He was Big Star and I was Little Star. Alluding to our stage performances I guess! My best friends were named Yellow Feather and her sister Babbling Brook! I remember the bravery challenge. We filled our mouths with water and had to keep silent walking around the entire park. Then at the end of the journey we spit out the water onto the ground proving our warrior capabilities. Babbling Brook couldn't do it. She couldn't keep quiet for more than a few moments and ended up swallowing her water.

My Grandfathers

My Grandfather, Fati was a chemical engineer and a Forman of a textile factory, Solvay back in Czechoslovakia. When they came to Chicago he worked for a while as a chemical engineer. My brother Darwin tells me he really didn't talk to the children and addressed him for the first time right before we moved from California to Indiana when Darwin was twelve years old. My mother told me she kept me away from him because he might have fondled some young girls. She didn't trust him either. I vaguely remember he had crazy eyebrows that reached out and molested the air in every direction. My dad told me about the licking he got probably more than once from this man. Maybe he got beat because he and his brother had stood on the roof and peed onto the "slechnow" or nanny.

My mom's dad, Grandpa David, died very young from heart disease. My mom was only in her twenties. She described him as being older than my Grandma. My Grandma called him Papa. I know Grandma had multiple abortions in the back alley and my mother was almost another one but lived because my Grandma was too sick with her gallbladder to have the abortion. They were very poor and worried about more mouths to feed. They lived in the Bronx, New York and my Grandpa David, worked on maintaining the trains as a brake inspector. He would come home after working swing shift and my mom would wait up for him and they would have a very late dinner together after my mom studied and did her homework. My mom seemed to always be on the swing shift and going to bed very late throughout her life. She even had me go to afternoon kindergarten so she could get me there on time.

Speaking of time, I learned to tell time well before my classmates in first grade. This was before everything was digital of course. When my teacher said that we would learn how to tell time I was excited and got up wanting to tell the class how to tell time. The teacher yelled at me, "SIT BACK DOWN!!!" So much for public education! Excitement for learning and teaching others was not appropriate. We were to sit and play dumb like good little children. I started writing with my left hand when we were learning how to print our letters. The teacher switched me to my right hand. I always felt like I did

something wrong when I
touched something or did
something with my left hand. It
developed where I would have
to go back and do it with my
right hand to make it ok and
decrease my anxiety.

My Brothers

We were raised by guilt. If we misbehaved my dad would say we were causing my mother stress, which was apparently a lethal condition. As it was my Grandma on my mom's side did die from a stroke caused apparently by stress. "YOUR KILLING YOUR MOTHER!!!" was the battle cry. Had my mother died when I was young I would have believed it was my fault. My mom drank coffee and taken allergy pills and started to hyperventilate from the combination. Her hands were curling in and she couldn't talk. I was home for lunch in second grade. Terrified I ran out of the house with an apron around my neck and a cheese sandwich clutched in my hand. I ran across the street and rang the doorbell and then back across the street and rang the doorbell next door. Mrs. Bleet came out and saw me in panic. "My mommy is sick." I managed to articulate. She called an ambulance and then came right over to take care of my mother. When the ambulance had taken my mom away Mrs. Bleet took me to her house where she allowed me to play with Jessi's big Barbie head and put make up on it and fix her hair! I didn't have one of those. My dad came to pick me up later. I was worried about being raised by only my dad.

My brother Harold became a second mother to me as he was told to "Take care of your sister!" When one of the kids in the neighborhood picked on me, Harold gave me a big stick to carry around with me. When the other kids saw me coming with it, they ran away!

Harold controlled the snowdrifts too. The snow was very beautiful during the winters in Indiana. Harold was concerned I shouldn't play and wreck the snowdrifts! He made paths around the snowdrifts that I was allowed to travel on and designated a specific area for me to play in and wreck the snow. My brothers got a crazy idea of making an ice-skating rink in our yard once. They

shoveled out a big area of the
snow and filled it with water.
They both ended up getting sick.
We did go ice-skating on the
Columbian Park pond when it
was frozen over in the winter.
My whole family skated. I had
my brother's sled, no ice-skates
for me. I remember zooming on
the sled full speed ahead across
the pond headed directly toward
my mother! I had no ability to
stop! I tried to scream but
nothing came out of my mouth. I
rammed square into her legs
and she fell directly on top of
me. I was compressed and got
the wind knocked out of me. My
mom had more stress than she
needed. But she made it to 82
years old! She passed away in
2009.

Harold became very good at keeping me in line in an imaginative sort of way. He told me when we were with mom in the department store that all the manikins were once real people. They did something wrong or misbehaved and were permanently frozen in that position. He had stories of how they got into the position they were displaying! Each dummy had a story behind them. I didn't want to be frozen so I was a very good girl when we went shopping. Harold was very good at organizing things. There was a specific order to the way the groceries were placed into the cart. One didn't just throw things into the shopping cart!

Eggs of course had to go on top so they wouldn't be crushed.

These were simpler times. The three of us would sit on the tailgate of my mom's rambler with the garage door open and watch the rainstorm for entertainment. We didn't need to be plugged into anything. My brother Darwin was an observer. He would be the one to point things out and notice detail. He was also knowledgeable and would give information. "See those clouds over there? They're heavier, darker and thicker than the other clouds. The scientific name for them is Nimbostratus." Darwin liked to read. Not only did my mom read to me but my brother Darwin read to me as well. He read "The Little Prince" to me and other philosophical type books. He made me think thoughts I never thought of thinking.

"Struwwelpeter" was a German Fairy Tale book Darwin read to me. It depicted a small child who had the habit of sucking his thumb. A man in the book called "Der Schnitter" or "The Cutter" pranced in and cut off the child's thumbs leaving him bleeding! Being an avid thumb sucker until at least age twelve, I was horrified. I feared getting my thumbs cut off by the Der Schnitter from Struwwelpeter almost as much as I feared Dracula biting my neck at night. I slept with the covers over my head.

My Pets

Back in California we had a cat named Bootsie and a rabbit named Hopper. I don't remember them. My mom did a woodcut print of them in black and white. I have the print hanging in my hallway today. In Indiana, we lived in a house on Kiowa Drive until I was in third grade. My mom brought home a cat that she found on the way home from a dinner party. It got sick and threw up and had diarrhea behind the toilet in the downstairs bathroom on Kiowa Drive. At least it knew the area to dump its load. My mom spent the rest of the day scrubbing the bathroom. While she was cleaning, my brothers and I entertained the cat with a string. Later that evening the cat was returned from whence it came. I was disappointed. I liked cats. I must have been three years old when I ran outside completely naked to say hello to a neighbor cat on the front porch. "Hello kitty!!!" There was a freedom in running around without clothes on. There were two games Harold and I played. One was "Naked Old Man and Jimmy." I would be under the covers naked. I was Jimmy. I thought I was a little boy. Harold told me that mine hadn't grown in yet! Later once I realized I was a girl,

I got poked in the left breast by him and he said that this one wouldn't grow. Amazingly my left breast is much smaller and the nipple is introverted!

We also played "Went To Zoo and Saw A..." were after Harold had a bath and was wrapped in his towel he would come down the hallway to my room next to his were I was in bed. He would hold up a towel open in front of him and say "Went To Zoo and Saw A..." I would then call out different animals and he would act them out. "Monkey!" He would say, "woo woo woo!" "Horse" He would say, "Neigh Neigh Neigh!" This could go on quite some time until I would say, "Daddy!" Then he would pretend to be

angry and say, "GO TO BED!!!!"
and the game would be over.

The Next Chapter

Jip Lockmore was my little
friend across the street. We
were about four years old and
he pointed a finger at me and
yelled, "YOU KILLED JESUS!" I
was developing a concept for
being Jewish. My family was
different in Lafayette, Indiana.
We were Jews not WASPS. In
first grade, they asked me to
stand in front of the class and
tell them about "The Jewish
Christmas." I remember sitting
in front of the class telling them
about lighting candles for
Hanukah and playing Dreidel...a

game where you spin a top
which has Hebrew letters on it. I
had Hebrew lessons and could
read Hebrew before I could read
English. I never learned to
translate Hebrew. I can sound it
out when reading it but I don't
know what it says!

Jip played with his little
Jewish friend just fine most of
the time and it wasn't an issue.
We played with Hot Wheel cars.
I got stuck in very tight shorts
one day. I must have been
growing like a weed. I couldn't
get my shorts down in time to sit
on the toilet and ended pooping
on the rug in the bathroom. Jip
called out to his mom, "HEIDI
DID GRUNNY ON THE FLOOR!" I
was mortified and ran home

crying leaving my Hot Wheel car behind.

I played with the older girls in the neighborhood too. Playing house, or school or Barbie was popular. I wanted a Barbie doll to dress up. I had trolls. It wasn't good for my self-esteem to have a troll to dress up and my friends had Barbie dolls! I would go over to where they were playing and ask the stupid question, "Can I play with you?" I was ignored. Nobody responded. They were being mean. So, I ran home crying to mommy. I kept asking for a Barbie doll. I was maybe five or six. I think my mom didn't think Barbie dolls were appropriate having breasts and hour glass figures. During Hanukah Harold and I were squeezing packages in the Hanukah basket. I felt a plastic container. I was convinced this was a Barbie doll!!! I was so excited!!! That evening when I opened it I discovered it was a hairbrush!!! I had a meltdown, hissy fit, and temper tantrum. I got a spanking from my mom with the hairbrush! Happy Hanukah Heidi!!! I did get a Barbie doll later when I was around twelve years old and didn't play with Barbie's anymore!

I was the only one in the neighborhood who had a Raggedy Andy though with a music box inside! My brother Darwin took an indelible green marker and put a mark on its forehead. "Now he's a Hindu."

He told me. I did brain surgery on him to remove the mark so he was permanently scared. We played house with the Raggedies. I had a little playhouse in the back yard and a jungle gym. I played the father and I would go to work by being on the jungle gym and pretending that I was driving a truck.

I actually did go to work with my father. I watched him dissect mice in the laboratory. He did cancer research in immunology. He was a clinical Biochemist. The mice kidneys looked just like kidney beans. I couldn't eat kidney beans for years after that. During one of my visits to my Dad's lab in the hospital one of my crayons broke. He taped it back together and told me that in the hospital things are fixed. I think I've always been comfortable in hospitals since then. I never thought of being a nurse when I was younger, but it seemed very natural for me to go into nursing later.

Lemonade stands were common for the kids in the neighborhood to do. They would charge ten cents a cup and make some change to go buy candy. I was told by my mom to sell mud pies for a leaf or two. The other kids came over expecting something. When I gave them a bowel of dirt they looked at me as if I were crazy. I'm selling them for a leaf! Ok, so much for imagination in that neighborhood. Mostly blue collar worker families...After third grade when I moved to the other side of town near Purdue University I was playing with professor's kids. Around age ten or eleven I had a friend Lena, who would sit on the picnic table in the back yard all afternoon with me. She was Tom Sawyer and I was Huckleberry Fin floating down the Mississippi River on our raft. I had friends that created different worlds in our minds. Jason and Karen would run around the neighborhood with me imagining we were two inches high in a game of "Little People." The trees became grass blades and a broom handle became a toothpick sword. We had names like Atoss and Miffel. Politically we had the Mouse-a-crates vs. the Rat-publicans. Both Jason and Karen were two years older than I. I couldn't understand when they started coming up with excuses like "I have to wash my hair today or practice for the fife and drum core," and not wanting to come out and play!

I was in both Brownies and then Girl Scouts. My mom was the leader in Brownies. I didn't wear my uniform to one meeting but instead a purple pants suit with a little lion pin pinned onto it. She said I looked like I was a member of the Purple Lion's Club not a Brownie.
Back in my first elementary school on the east side of

Lafayette prior to third grade we had to wear dresses to school. When I moved to West Lafayette where Purdue University was we were allowed to wear pants in school. I enjoyed the freedom of pants. They were more practical for running and playing than dresses. When I did wear a dress, I would wear shorts underneath. By doing this, if your dress flew up you were safe.

It was in the fifth grade that I got my period at ten and a half eleven years old. My mom being an artist drew pictures and described very well what I would be going through. She was very concerned that it wouldn't happen to me and me not knowing what it was. As a young girl my mom got her first period when she was in the movie theater bathroom. She thought she was dying and went home to go to bed. When she told her aunt the only explanation that she got was, "The Queen of England does it too honey." My mom would talk to me about the summers she spent in Belmar, New Jersey with her Aunt Jenine. Aunt Jenine would rent out rooms in a big boarding house. My mom would be sent there to get out of the city for the summer. My Grandma and Aunt Jenine would be having tea in the kitchen and send my mom upstairs to "play with" Andrew. My mom's cousin Andrew was fifteen years old. My mom was only five. He took her up to the attic and as my mom would tell me "look from where her legs were growing." He also had his boyfriends come and mess around with her. She hated Andrew. He apparently did this to her for years while unaware adults sat sipping tea in the kitchen. He eventually gave my mom a wooden easel for her artwork as a proposal gift. She refused to marry him but took that easel everywhere we moved. After my dad died in 2005 she moved in with me. Here came the old wooden easel off the moving truck. I handed my mom an axe and said, "Chop it up mom!" She couldn't do it. "Well someone might use it someday," She replied. Today it sits in our living room clinic

with a white board on it. My
brother Darwin uses it to
instruct and teach people who
come to our Energy Medicine
Clinic every Wednesday evening
at 7:30pm. I guess my mom
would be happy we are getting
use out of it. Most of her anger
came out in her artwork. She
had a castration complex going
on. Soft sculpture Raggedy
Adam and Raggedy Eve had
Adam with detachable parts.
She had a big Styrofoam
sculpture called "The Ovary
Machine." The Styrofoam little
white squiggly things used for
packing where the eggs coming
out of the red tunnel like
ovaries.
She had made a woodcut of
Salome in the bible carrying the

severed head of John the Baptist. She expressed herself through her artwork. She used her creativity in many ways. She covered the bathroom door with cut outs of flowers to hide the holes that Darwin had punched in them with his expression of anger. Harold was chasing me. I was screaming and ran into the bathroom and jumped into the tub. Darwin was chasing Harold. Harold ran into the bathroom after me and shut the door. Darwin's fist came through the door after Harold! We kept pretty busy creating stress for my mom.

My mom encouraged my creativity. She allowed me to draw on the unfinished basement walls in crayon and was always introducing me to new media like paper Mache to make things like puppet heads and clay to make whatever I wanted to create. She taught classes at the Lafayette Art Center. I modeled for some of her art classes wearing a leotard when I was nine or ten years old. I got to use the art supplies there, as well as in my mom's studio at home. My mom and dad were also involved in the Civic Theater in Lafayette, Indiana. My mom acted as well as designed stage sets and my dad built the stage sets. I was able to participate and play a village child. I remember the song to the Snow Queen. The kids sang: WE LIKE TO WORK IN A GARDEN. TO TEACH THE

SEEDS HOW TO GROW. TO
TEACH THE BUDS HOW TO
BLOSSOM. TO PLANT THEM ALL
IN A ROW! DON'T ASK THE
REASON WE LIKE THESE
THINGS THERE IS JUST NO
RULE TO APPLY. YOU LIKE THE
THINGS YOU LIKE AND THERE
IS NOONE TO TELL YOU WHY!
My mom played a Gypsy in Snow
Queen and her song went like
this: COME AND HAVE YOUR
FORTUNES TOLD AND MEET
THE GYPSY BAND! I CAN READ
THE TEA LEAVES OR THE PALM
OF ANY HAND! I CAN SEE
TOMORROW WHEN I GO INTO A
TRANCE! COME AND HAVE
YOUR FORTUNES TOLD…COME
AND TAKE A CHANCE!!! She
lifted her skirt and banged

together the symbols tied onto
her knees!

I became very good at creating
characters too. By ten or eleven
years old I was speaking to my
mom mostly through puppets.
She yelled at me once, "I WANT

TO TALK TO **YOU** NOT TO YOUR
HAND!" I had special funny
voices I would use and funny
expressions. BaBa was one of
them. Maybe because I'm an
Aries or just a really good
sheeple...BaBa sticks with me
today.

My roommates call me BaBa. I have an animation of this character as well. I think she is just as cute if not cuter than Hello Kitty. I think BaBa should be famous like Hello Kitty. I use to drive my mom nuts with the characters. I would parade around naked in front of her singing the BaBa song. Yes, this sounds a little weird. My mom and I were very close. She was my best friend in Junior High. I would crawl into my parent's bed after my Dad left for work and we would "cuddle schmuddle." My mom usually slept late being on swing shift and my dad would make breakfast and get us ready for school. Breakfast was always a hardboiled egg, cereal, milk and an orange cut up in quarters. My dad was very consistent that way. Usually there was time after my dad left for work before we went off to school. I started with the zit squeezing rituals by age twelve or thirteen. Every little bump on my face had to be squeezed and emptied before I would make it to school. Sometimes I would be an hour late and my face all blotchy. I felt ugly. I had braces on my teeth and was gawky and awkward. One day I came home in pain from my braces being tightened. I was crying and couldn't eat anything. My dad was home and made me a milkshake! He had his moments! When he learned that I got my period he gave me a plant with pink flowers! I named the plant Menstruate! My creativity was developing. In school I made a paper Mache duck with a sailor hat on. He was quite famous and was displayed in the principal's office for a while. His name was Moby Duck! I got into my first fistfight in Junior High. Darwin had been studying the martial arts and taught me how to defend myself. I was challenged to a "duel" by one of my girlfriends. She said four in the afternoon after school next Monday. I said why? You need to practice? What is the matter with right now? She threw the first punch and I caught her arm and twisted it around like my brother had showed me. I was sent to the guidance counselor who happened to be a piece of eye candy. A young man named Mr. Milner. I developed a crush on him. My mom and I would sing: OH MR MILNER...WE LOVE YOU...OH MR MILNER...YES WE DO...WHEN YOU ARE NEAR US..WE ARE BLUE! OH, MR MILNER WE LOVE YOU! I saw Mr. Milner regularly after that. He was like my first therapist. Before that my mom heard about everything I experienced in life. Now I had a new pair of listening ears! Mr. Milner thought it was a good idea for me to see him since my dad had lost his job. I guess I had been acting out the stress at home.

To my dismay between seventh and eighth grade after my Bat Mitzvah in Augusts we moved up to Chicago where my dad had a new job. My mom picked a very Jewish area, Highland Park, where I **really** did not fit in!

Chicago

A new school, practically in my back yard! My mom thinking it would be cute gave me a red shirt with the words "**NEW KID**" on it to wear the first day of school. I was dumb enough to wear it and was the target of humiliation. I ended up in a wrong classroom. They called my name to come to the office as they were trying to find me and instead of walking out the door to go to the office I walked into the closet. The class was in hysterics. I was afraid to come out of the closet once I walked in and stayed in there long enough for the class of adolescents to be completely out of control. I eventually found my way to the right class. I stopped by the counselor's office to talk. Her name was Miss Crudette and was old enough to have been Mr. Milner's mother! Since they did not have an orchestra for me to continue playing the Viola she signed me up for the basketball team. I was tall but still uncoordinated. The short captain of the team, Jade Warren, had a field day tormenting me. Her two bodyguards, Willy Wooly and Bobby Bibber, protected her. I had to share a locker with one of Jade's friends Sandra Tempberg. She treated me as a less than too. I didn't have the right labels on my clothes. "WHAT no Adidas tennis shoes!!! Where did you get those? K-MART!!!" I soon moved into my friend from the basketball team's locker. Her name was Anna. Her father was in the military at fort Sheridan. She had a lot of brothers and sisters and moved around quite a bit. I liked her, as she was not at all pretentious. I didn't leave Sandra's locker quietly either. I strung up a bucket of water on the shelf and connected it to the door. When Sandra opened the locker the next morning SPLASH! As the Northwood Junior High newspaper read, "Niagara Falls, Falls Again!" I was an adolescent. Acting out!

I started High School and signed up for acting classes! I was tall and thin with short dark hair. I caught the eye of my acting instructor. She showed me some special attention on my first day of class. She told me to wear the same red shirt (not the New Kid shirt!) the next day so she would remember me. The

next day I wore a blue shirt. She
laughed and was joking about
me wearing a blue shirt instead.
I copped an attitude suddenly. I
was defensive and said she was
"picking on me." I regret that.
She showed her favorites special
attention. She never showed me
that attention again. I tried out
for play after play and never
made the cast list. I helped back
stage and ended up picking up
bear hands full of scrambled egg
off the stage floor that the kid
playing Helen Keller had spewed
out of her mouth. Gross. I tried
out for every play and didn't
make any except for being in the
pub scene in Oliver Twist. I
upstaged Fagan having my mom
doing my makeup and having
my teeth blacked out! I carried a

rubber chicken with me and practicing sense memory had just come out of the "kitchen" to sing oom-pa-pa! By senior year I hadn't made any significant part. I tried out yet again. When the cast list went up on the Acting Department bulletin board I saw I wasn't on it. I wrote a nice little poem for the acting teacher: MAY SHE DO WELL ON HER NEXT SUPER SHOW WHICH WILL BE GODSPELL!

No one would suspect me. I was a good kid. I got good grades. I was nice to people for the most part. I even went to my guidance counselor and told him I was BURNING mad that I didn't make the cast list. Nobody suspected me...I set the cast list on fire! I heard someone yell fire as I ran out the back door, the callboard going up in flames. I dumped all my matches outside under a bush. Waved "hello" to a few people I knew outside The Glass Hall, which changed to The Brick Hall as so many students had thrown each other through the glass. I circled the building and came in through the front door. I was never suspected or caught. The following year I saw that the bulletin board was replaced with a glass case. The future cast lists were put inside an enclosed case for safe display! The only thing I remember getting in trouble for at school was drawing cartoons on the desk top in pencil in my math class. My math teacher had me wash off the top of the desk.

I was a good kid, with an acting out streak when I was unhappy about something!

When I was in High School Muti had just lost Fati and my dad brought her from California to come to live with us. My brother Harold was home most of the day practicing his violin for various performances. Muti

drove him crazy. She was always
disturbing his practice accusing
the caregiver we got for her was
doing "Hanky Panky" with my
brother! She would run away
multiple times. We couldn't keep
a caregiver. The last straw
happened when she ran off to
Israel and we got a long-distance
call from a taxi driver to go pick
her up! After this my dad
decided to place her in a locked
nursing home facility. By this
time, I was learning to drive.
Darwin went with me to obtain
my driver's license. During the
hands-on driving test the
instructor told me to put my
directional on. I just sat there
with a blank look. Darwin was
standing outside the car and
laughed! "She calls it a blinker!

Put your blinker on, Heidi!" I
immediately understood what
the instructor wanted and
complied. Darwin laughs about
"the blinker" incident event to
this day! I practiced driving with
my dad next to me on the Eden's
Expressway going to visit Muti.
She had stabbed a nurse with a
pair of scissors thinking that the
nurse was stealing from her.
They were not very happy with
her. My mom and I took her out
to the mall once and she got this
very pale make up. It made her
look sick. I think that was the
intent. I think she starved
herself to death. We didn't do
funerals in my family. Fati had
been donated to Science. He was
in a pickle jar at UCLA. Muti was
cremated. We had a memorial

service in our living room and
Harold and I couldn't stop
laughing. We were having
hysterics. Anything serious, we
couldn't cope. Passover Harold
would change the words or act
out gesturing and get me to
laugh so hard I would pee in my
pants. At least Passover we were
drunk on Manischewitz wine! I
don't know what our excuse was
at Muti's memorial service. My
dad had episodes of depression.
He would be weepy and
melancholy at times. As I got
older I remember he was tearful
at times and apologized for
"being such a terrible father." I
always felt I had to protect him.
"You're not a terrible father!" I
replied. He always provided for
us and did not abandon us like

so many other fathers have done.   One thing he taught me that really sticks with me is the Law of the 7 Ps. I use this frequently; "proper program planning prevents pitiful piss poor performance." Actually, there are 8 Ps. It's is kind of like the nursing process: Assessment, Diagnosis, Plan, Intervention and Evaluation. I would come up with some of my own sayings as well. I entered college with the inquisitive attitude, "Answer my question and I'll question your answer!" My dad also taught me "the only constant thing in life is change!" He wanted me to be adaptable and flexible despite whatever plans I was making. He encouraged my independence.

Dad would point out that he and mom would not be around forever and I needed to make a living and be capable of supporting myself. I was not encouraged to major in acting in college even though I loved my acting class in High School and wanted to be an actress. Dad insisted I take chemistry, physics and math in High School because I would need them later in life. Although acting helped me tremendously come out of my mommy hanging shyness and had an impact on my life, I was encouraged to focus on the sciences in High School. I enjoyed biology. My teacher Mr. Einbot had a real snake in the room and I touched a reptile for the first time and found it wasn't slimy like I had thought it would be! It was leathery. My mom had snake phobia and every time a snake came up in a movie or on TV she would hyperventilate. When my brother Darwin put a raccoon tail on his high school graduation cap instead of his tassel it was as if my mom had seen ten thousand snakes crawling on her and had a mock coronary. I thought the running out of the house holding a cheese sandwich incident was upsetting. When my mom saw Darwin and his raccoon tail she spazzed out! She had a conniption fit. For some reason, because we were in Lafayette, Indiana where there weren't many Jewish people, somehow this act made us, as Jews, look bad?!

My mom use to say that Grandma would yell at her when she was a child, "WHAT WILL THE NEIGHBORS THINK!?" I learned that the neighbors and anyone else could judge us and we should adjust our behavior accordingly. I'm unlearning this. I'm sure our neighbor today being a psychiatrist probably thinks from all the sound Qi Gong, grunting from yoga, hysterical laughter and drum circle clopping that we are all completely nuts over here. I have two great roommates and Darwin lives with me as well. I will get into my present life later. My point is. I've had to relearn to not have to please people all the time, including neighbors! Part of the reason I mention this is because I've suffered greatly and unnecessarily worrying about what other people think. If I were to continue to be concerned about what other people would think I would have never started to write this book! I continue to write despite headaches and back pain. Writing is a good distraction and I remain focused and on a mission.

My brother Harold always had focus when it came to playing the violin. He was highly influenced by the Amadeus Mozart Quartet and their first violinist Peter Schidlof. My dad had met Peter Schidlof in the internment camp in England. Later when I was about four years old they came to visit us in Lafayette in the house on Kiowa Dive. Harold combed my hair like one of the quartet members, Siggy. He parted my, at the time very short, hair in the middle and combed it back on either side. I remember Peter's face had spots on it like the icing on the orange muffins my mom made. I looked at him and started wailing and nobody knew why. I had an orange muffin in front of me and didn't want to eat his face. Harold watched in wonder as the musicians played. Soon after as he was in fifth grade he started playing the violin and practiced scratching on it for hours. I got used to it and listened quietly as his scratching became music! Darwin however, liked the peace and quiet so he could study. To him I was a loud mouth brat. Harold and I disturbed his nirvana and serenity. Harold and I made fun of him calling Darwin "A big fat Gazebo." We thought that sounded good but we were calling him "A big fat out door garden structure!!!" Kids are very funny in their use of language sometimes. I use to say Brefgits instead of Breakfast and Aminals instead of animals! I once philosophically asked at age five while sitting in the bathtub, "Is that big guy God going to put me up his pot?" What I meant was that I saw God as a baldheaded Boy Scout leader who made people in pots in Heaven's kitchen. I guessed after he made us we lived our lives until it was time to go back into his pot?! I was asking about death. Pretty advanced thinking for a five-year-old, nobody really understood me, my family laughed about "Is that big guy God going to put me up his pot." for years. My family defiantly practiced rites of passage. I remember when I was finished using baby bottles at age three we had a big parade and marched through the entire house with me in the lead carrying my baby bottles! At the end of the parade we stopped in front of the trashcan and I threw out my baby bottles. My mom use to get me to eat things I didn't like by making a face with the food. "Now just eat Witchipoo's radish eyes and try some of the tomato ear! I had a good appetite though and usually ate the carrot nose and rice and pea mixture mouth. The ground hamburger meat hair was the first to go.

Speaking of hair my mom got tired of fighting with all my curls by age four. Especially when I started nursery school and she didn't have time to mess with it. So, the solution she found was to have my hair cut extremely short. My mom had short hair too but her hair was fine and easy to manage. My short thick curly hair tweaked out in funny directions. My bangs were way too short and my mom stood over me while I got my hair cut to make sure they cut the bangs short so that they wouldn't impede my vision. The first haircut was very traumatic. I cried of course. My mom saved some of the hair and I have a lock of it all curled up in my Doo Dad Box. That's a box where I keep things like removed braces from my teeth or planter's warts that were cut out of the bottom of my foot! I still have my Doo Dad Box! I started to grow my hair out again junior year in High School.

My brothers usually babysat for me when my parents went out for the evening. Darwin was in charge and Harold made dinner. I remember TV dinners in the metal trays; Salisbury steak, mashed potatoes and peas. Harold started making simple things like spaghetti too. He eventually turned out to be a decent cook. When my parents went a long trip, they left this old lady in charge. She sat around watching TV most of the time. Harold made me lunch but when I came home to eat it the old lady had eaten the nice lunch Harold had made. The three of us were pretty upset with her un-involvement and tried to call my parent's long distance to see if we could fire her! When my brothers were much older and busy with school mom and dad got a young college couple to live-in and baby-sit for me when they went to Bermuda. I was maybe in Junior High. The man, Charlie used to tell me stories. He was very animated telling me a story of "The Big Mouth Frog." Darwin was studying or working being an ambulance driver. Harold was probably practicing his violin. Charlie and his wife Amy were available and great company.

My mom started teaching art after I started High School. We were already in the Chicago area living in Highland Park. We were close and one day my mom came in with her used sanitary napkin. On it was a perfect heart shaped blood spot! This was something that she could not share with my brothers or my dad! My mom talked to me quite a bit about Cousin Andrew in the attic. This she couldn't share with my brothers or dad either. When I was in High School my mom and I would take the train down to Chicago and go the museums. She took me to the Thorn room exhibit back when we still lived in Indiana. These were miniature rooms filled with miniature objects and furniture. I loved it! I was heavily into trolls. Jason liked to play with trolls when I was in sixth grade. We would sit for hours making clothes out of rectangle pieces of cloth. Jason even sewed little snaps on rather than have the stylish safety pin look! We would build shoebox houses and I would make tiny books for their library. I even found a little miniature phone and record player for my trolls. My cousin Lenora gave most of my trolls to me. My mom's sister had a child with muscular dystrophy. She died when she was 21. I was still a baby. She had been a very good artist. I have a picture she painted of Winken, Blinken and Knodd in their wooden shoe boat hanging in my room. She gave it to my mom for me and it has always had a place in my room. Funny I always loved animation and cartoons. I painted a mural of the tortoise and the hare in my friend's children's room with all the animals waving them on at the finish line, which was the closet door. One could break through the finish line by folding the side-by-side closet doors open from the middle. I also did a mural around my cousin Aleena's pool. The mural depicted ocean creatures. All the caricatures in my murals are cute and animated. I learned appreciation for art and enjoyed going to Chicago for the art exhibits and of course I went because afterward would be the colossal "Lake Front" Ice cream Sunday at Marshal Fields Crystal Palace!!! Mom and I would skip dinner that day. I kid you not. The Sunday came in a glass the size of a large fruit tray. I ate the whole thing by myself! Frango Mint and all! Of course, I am an Aries with a ferocious appetite! Mom was always buying me gifts. If I showed them to my dad he would say, "You have a rich mother, don't you?" I think maybe he was angry about her spending his money. My brother Darwin lived at home through college. He only left home because we moved up to Chicago and he stayed in West Lafayette to work on his PhD at Purdue University. I got the idea from my dad that he didn't want me to be dependent on him and me hanging around.

I was sixteen years old and my dad asked me to turn on the dishwasher. I asked him which button? He started slapping me in my face and yelling, "TURN IT ON...TURN IT ON... TURN IT ON". I decided I would leave home at that point. I had had enough. The next morning I packed my school bag with things I thought I would need and took off. I went down town by train as I had done many times before with my mom. I knew where the train station was because we used to come in from West Lafayette, Indiana to there. I had enough money from babysitting kids in the neighborhood that I bought a Greyhound Ticket back to West Lafayette, Indiana and ended up on Darwin's doorstep! I was obviously disturbing him. "Why are you here? You need to go home." He called mom and dad. They told him to send me back. When I arrived home, I received both hysteria and aloofness, "How dare you make us worry!!!" I made a point of saying to my dad at great risk that I got to Indiana by myself and I didn't crap in my pants like he said he thought I would. He just said. "Couldn't you think of another way?" No. At that point I made a stab at independence. I wasn't hanging onto my mom. I wanted to be out on my own. That summer I went to Las Vegas to stay with my Aunt Heather. She just lost her husband my Uncle Leon, my mom's brother. I was to keep her company and I would still have a mother type to look after me. I ended up staying most of the time with her children. My cousin, Danny, who was a little older than Darwin, had a wife and kids. He worked as a pit boss at Caesar's Palace. He had connections and got me my first real job as a junior camp counselor at a Jewish day camp. I was seventeen and had eleven and twelve-year-old kids. The senior counselor was a nineteen-year-old guy who was very cool with the kids. We all went to see "The Empire Strikes Back" as a camp trip. I took care of Danny's little four-year-old Raymond. Raymond was a wise old man in a child's body. He and I would have very in depth discussions sitting on the basketball court in the park near-by. He would take after his dad and say clever things like, "You know dad. I like his face!" Raymond and I were waiting in the casino for Danny and Raymond took a quarter he found and put it in a quarter slot machine. I had to help him pull the lever down because he was small. He won the jackpot!!!! It must have been around $27. Danny came home from Caesars at 2:00AM. He put Raymond in the car and he and his wife took me to Disneyland for the first time!!! Raymond woke up when we got to the park. He went to sleep in his bed in Las Vegas and woke up in Disneyland Parking lot!!! There at Disneyland Raymond bought a huge at least three feet tall stuffed Donald Duck with it!!! One of Raymond's ears on his mouse hat came off so his dad called him "Mono-ear!" after the monorail. Danny's wife got really upset with me for hanging my laundry out on the balcony to dry. This was uncouth at the Disneyland Hotel! She sent my nice white Mickey Mouse t-shirt to the dry cleaners and it came back gray! Danny got really upset with me when I lost patience with Raymond. After Raymond spit a mouth full of pool water on me when I was sunbathing I freaked out like the raging Hulk and threw Raymond in the pool. He found his way to the edge and got out crying his way back to the hotel room. "What's the matter with you...you can talk to me you know." I hadn't learned yet to talk about feelings at that point and expressed myself through painting or acting out! My fear was expressed very clearly on my first rollercoaster, the Matterhorn! Danny sat in front of me and pried my fingers from his neck after the ride. He had red rings on his neck from my grip. I couldn't scream I was so scared. I just hung onto Danny's neck tighter.

I spent part of that summer in Las Vegas at my cousin Aleena's. She had two kids. I spent most of the time hanging out with Allen, Aleen's son, who was nine at the time. He is a lawyer today. Back then he had a tummy ache and needed to be comforted by his father after roller-skating around parking lots all day with me. We went with Dena his eleven-year-old sister (who watched Grease over a hundred times that summer) to the water slides. I was out in the hot Las Vegas summer sun all day and when we got to Aleena's I was seeing my peripheral vision turn gray and felt like passing out. I had sunstroke. Aleena felt red meat would help. We had steaks that night. I recovered very quickly. One dinner at Aleena's we had lobster! That was my first time having lobster and I loved it! I was there over 4th of July and I was amazed at all the fireworks they had on that street. Aunt Heather was afraid Allen would singe his eyebrows off! He got very close to the fireworks to light them. I did some painting when I was there. Aleena was a cocktail waitress at The Maxim. She had left early evening. I had come in after painting after

4:00pm. Allen and Dena were over at friends. Aleen's husband Jack was there with some of his friends. He worked as a dealer in one of the casinos. He offered me a line of cocaine!!! I didn't want to take any drugs. I was concerned that it would mess up my brain chemistry. Between Darwin talking to me about situations he saw on the ambulance crew and teaching me about the brain and my dad's background as a Biochemist I was quite aware that drugs could mess you up. I refused. Later I stayed for a very short period with my cousin Penny. She was openly smoking pot and telling me that it opened the mind. I already got drunk one breakfast there because I didn't know the orange juice was spiked with vodka! Penny and her boyfriend took me to a party with them. This one guy with buckling knees and rotten teeth asked me, "Hey man...you want some Ludes?" I thought if that is what it does to me than no thank you! I probably could have easily started on drugs and been a drug addict there in Las Vegas at age seventeen, but I didn't have the need. I was a good student and I was looking forward to going to college. I had gotten in to Purdue University in West Lafayette, Indiana!!!! I was going back to my home where I grew up!

College

I had seen a mime show on campus and was very interested in doing mime. I went to their audition. All the mimes that had been in the mime show, were on the stage without their make-up. One of them asked us to each

stand up and individually
introduce ourselves. When it
was my turn and I said my name
behind me was a voice,
"Heidi???" It was my Junior High
and grade School friend, Lena
from the picnic table raft!!!! We
ended up performing in the Red
Brick Mime Troop through
college. We did shows for the
president's luncheons to the girl
scouts. Every semester we
would have all-new skits in a
new show. "Mime and
Pun-ishment!" "Once upon a
Mime!" "Sounds of Silence!" My
favorite joke was that I was on
the "props committee." Of
course, our skits were created
out of thin air from our
imagination! What props!!? On
campus, I saw several of my old

friends from Grade School. I
even saw Jason there still
playing in the fife and drum
core! He went to pharmacy
school. He set me up on a date
with his friend Arney Morton.
Arney was a total nerd and
totally into his world of science
and math. I was in engineering
and agriculture my first year. He
helped me study a little. We had
a kissing encounter right before
the first semester ended and we
went on vacation. He refused to
talk to me after we came back
and I guess we "broke up." I
didn't have too much time for
dating then anyway. I listened to
how much Elana Petrino, one of
the mimes in the mime troop
loved nursing school! I applied
to get into Nursing. It tied

together all the subjects that I was really interested in; Biology, Sociology, Psychology and I could take as many Humanities classes as I wanted to. I took sign language as my language requirement. I was having dreams in sign language and mime!

We did mime out on the mall playing with people on campus. There was a preacher named Max who use to run after us pointing to us screaming, "YOU...YOU in the whiteface! SINNER!!!" This just egged us on more and we would prance around silently laughing at him. We learned once the greasy zinc oxide base covers your face you remain silent. With one exception, there was a small child jumping up and down on my foot and kicking me while I was doing street mime at the market square. I held her arm and looked her in the face and said in a low voice said, "Stop jumping on my foot!" She was shocked that I spoke. It probably traumatized her for life! She ran away crying.

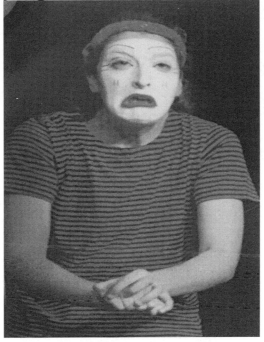

So, the following year I was a sophomore at college but really a freshman in Nursing School. We had to wear the hats derived from nun habits until they were canned my Junior year in Nursing School for multiple reasons but mainly because we were getting males into Nursing School and they didn't have to wear the hats! My class was the first Bachelor's program going through. Before our four-year Bachelor's program there was a two-year Associate Degree program that was done first. Then after you already had your RN license one could go another two years and get the Bachelor's Degree. We didn't sit for the licensing exam until after the four years. It was a program that was excellent in textbook and theory but most of us felt we didn't get enough clinical experience. There were also the three-year diploma students that were trained over at St. Elizabeth Hospital. They had a lot of experience in clinical practice but no degree.

PARRRTAY!

So, I was an excellent student and excelled in textbook and theory land, but I wasn't ready for the "Real World." I decided to study therapeutic interaction on my own, as I loved psychology and had a minor in psychology. I went into therapy at the student center. Seemed like the natural thing to do. I didn't have my guidance counselors in school to listen to me anymore. I really didn't think I had much in the way of serious problems. I embellished and acted quite dramatic initially so I could study the therapist's responses. I use to play psychiatrist with a friend of mine in High School. I would be the patient and she would be the psychiatrist. This was an opportunity to study a real professional. I was quite surprised the therapist maintained composure and had

a non-judgmental attitude!
Toward the end, I felt like I
didn't need to make anything
up! Just being me was ok! I told
her I was embellishing and even
that became a point of interest!
Why did I feel like I had to make
things up? When the therapist
went to the bathroom I snuck
into her file and pulled out my
record and stuck it in my
backpack to made copies of it
later. I wanted to see what she
wrote about me. I was curious.
She wrote I was a disturbed
woman! Really!? First, I was
now a woman...not "the Gehrrl"
I am now a WOMAN! New
concept. And I was disturbed!
Disturbed? The only thing in my
mind I was truly disturbed
about was not getting a good

grade. The fact that I wasn't graded in therapy was disturbing. Didn't I do it right? Was disturbed a good thing? I convinced the therapist I had a problem and now I was getting confused! I needed to continue this but I graduated and therapy was over!!!

I had multiple scholarships getting me through nursing school. One of them I had a commitment to work for Community Hospital in Indianapolis. I wasn't ready. They had no preceptor ship program or transitional immersion program for a new grad like most places have today. They just threw you out on the floor and when you did something wrong an older nurse would say, "We don't do it like that here Hun!" Before graduation I was wined and dined by an Air Force recruiter. They had money. I was given a leather bookmark and ceramic cup. I still have those items today. Sergeant Kalle, the recruiter described a nursing internship with the program where I could develop my nursing skills in a structured environment with supervision. I thought it would be awesome to be a flight nurse and do nursing up in the sky! If we did go to war I would be a nurse putting soldiers back together again. I thought I might go into surgical nursing. I had a vision of being a very competent well-trained nurse after the Air Force.

So, I had my swearing in
taking my Air Force oath with
the recruiter, Sergeant Kalle, in
the South Tower at Purdue
University where I went for
mime practice. This was a rite of
passage. I was leaving student
hood and becoming an Air Force
Officer. My dad was very proud
of me. My mom was freaked out

and did not want me to go. She was afraid I would be killed or that something would happen to me. A few of the mimes stayed after practice to witness the ceremony. We had cake and I felt excited as I was starting a new life. I didn't work at Community Hospital in Indianapolis more than a few days and was fired and freed of my scholarship commitment. At the time, I realized my decision to go into the Air Force for the nursing internship program was a good one. I had worked as a camp counselor and taught mime with the parks district through college. I didn't have a clue how the hospital system worked. I was not functioning in the capacity of a nurse. Patients were coming back from surgery. I could have easily identified the right answers on a test but to take off doctor's orders and monitor patients... I just stood there! Things were happening around me at a very fast pace and I was not able to get what I was supposed to do. Before I went to the Air Force Military Indoctrination for Medical Officers, two-week party how to wear your uniform and salute, I worked at another hospital, a fabric store and a nursing home. I needed the Internship Program. I was also looking forward to being stationed out in California! I was supposed to have my internship at March Air Force Base near Riverside California and be permanently stationed in Lompoc at Vandenberg Air Force Base. I was later rerouted to Edwards Air Force Base near Lancaster, California instead of Vandenberg.

Before going into the military I worked briefly at Riley Children's Hospital in infant critical care. Another very fast pace where babies changed fast and you had to be on your toes. They at least had a preceptor who most the time ignored me until I gave a bottle of formula to a baby who had stitches in his abdomen. I wasn't supposed to feed the baby more than 30 cc of formula. It was so hungry it took the whole bottle before I even thought about it. The baby was ok but I was fired. I was thinking

I should try something other than nursing and worked for a day learning to cut fabric in a sewing store. Then I got a nice slow paced job in Americana Nursing Home. There was an LVN in charge who had lots of experience. My job was to pass medications down the long hallway on each patient. Then I would go back down the hallway and take my dinner break then start passing bedtime medications. I leaned my arm into nitroglycerine cream on a patch and it vasodilated my blood vessels and I passed out! I was very much ok with the LVN being in charge and enjoyed the job! There was a family of one man who died from cancer. They appreciated the care that I gave him and gave me a Cabbage Patch Doll, which looked like me! Another man's hands used to shake; I would fill his water glass half full so he wouldn't spill it. He looked at me and said, "A bit stingy with your water ain't ya?!" I sat with him when he was dying. He was concerned his wife was still alive in the bed next to him and he was worried that he wouldn't be able to see her have a nice funeral. If he went before her he could not oversee things. We had eight people die in one week. I didn't mind sitting and talking with people and being there for them as they expired. There was a fire in the nursing home right before I started into the military. It happened on the shift before

me and everyone got out ok.
They transferred the patients to
another facility and I was
passing medications at the other
facility on 56 patients instead of
23 patients. I learned to be
organized.

Darwin came to visit me before I
went into the Air Force. I had an
apartment I shared with another
nurse and two-stuffed
handmade Avanti Lions! I
bought them with my very first
credit card. We had very little
furniture. Darwin's old couch
with a missing arm was in the
living room with my Lions. I had
a mattress to sleep on. I pretty
much sat cross-legged between
the two Lions and ate dinner. I
think Darwin had come just
after I had been fired from Riley

Children's Hospital. I cried on his shoulder. By the time, I was working in the Nursing Home I was settling into a routine. I had moved everything from college and my parent's house into this apartment. Everything I owned was under one roof. A few pots and pans from my mom, clothes, books and stuffed animals! The Air Force did not have a whole lot to move across country. The Air Force packed me up and moved my stuff. I had my orders and drove initially in my Renault Alliance (Rudy the Red Renault) with another nurse to MIMSO in Texas. We must have listened to the hit song "Don't Worry Be Happy" at least 100 times on the trip. It was January 1987. The Indiana winter chased us all the way to Texas. We had an ice storm that week and individual blades of grass were encapsulated in a shell of ice. The grass crunched when one walked on it! There was also a light snow and my co-officers and I made snow angels by lying on the ground and flapping our arms up and down in the snow thinking we might not be able to do this in sunny California. Our Red Flag training was cancelled because of the icy weather. I imagined Red Flag training and wrote a scenario that I presented at the final assembly. It was entitled "Medical Readiness Day."

Medical Readiness Day

The sound of my hot air popcorn popper whirred in my ears. I lay prone on my bed letting my imagination create visions of "Medical Readiness Day." As each "colonel" of corn exploded I heard high velocity ammunition whizzing past my ears. It hit the wall behind me tearing through the structure as if it were Jell-O. (We had viewed videos as part of our training on how different kind of ammunition rips through tissue like Jell-O.) I kept myself low and wriggled across the floor in my fatigue colored sweats. I had to fight my way through the thicket of my mind and the brambles of my ingenuity. There in front of me lay the colonel. There was a gaping wound in his side. Blood spurted from it. $K=MV2$, boy this one must have been going faster than the speed of light. Too bad this wasn't an NCO (Non-Commissioned Officer). He would have caught the bullet in his teeth and ate it. I gently turned the colonel over. It must have gone in his back. A tiny hole was barely visible. I ripped off my undergarments. Using the absorbent material, I applied pressure to the artery, which had been severed from the impact of the bullet.

Suddenly a string of bullets buzzed past me. Then a massive explosion burst through the air. It appears every gun on the opposing side was fired. How am I going to get out of here? I started to panic. I tried tugging at the colonel's fatigue suite hoping I could drag him along with me. I'm going to die I thought. I can't do that to my mother. I must live. I must help my unit. An overwhelming feeling overpowered all sensation and I froze. I heard nothing. I saw nothing. I knew nothing. My mind was playing tricks on me. There was a little girl standing before me with a dog. "Hi!" she said, "Can you tell me where the wizard is?" I couldn't move. I was frozen solid. I felt as stiff as a green bean from an MRE (meal ready to eat). I tried to scream for help, but found my neurons were unable to stimulate any of my muscles.

Three hours later my roommate walked in. "What are you doing on the floor, Heidi?" She questioned. "Smells like popcorn. May I have some?" Reality jarred my jam. The colonel in front of me was merely a kernel of corn, which had blown onto the floor. I had a sock wrapped around my hand pushing on the floor next to it. "Sure," I replied, "Help yourself! I was just picking up some popcorn that I dropped. How's the weather outside?" "It's still really cold and icy," she answered, "I guess it's good that they cancelled Medical Readiness."

I got a standing ovation for reading what I wrote on the last day. I was popular in a short period. Earlier I had written all the toasts for the formal dinner where we had to wear out dress blues. It wasn't acceptable for one person to write all the toasts because we had broken up into a group and we were all supposed to contribute. So, after I knocked off the poems we divided them up and each person in the group claimed one.

Toasts

Cheers to all from MIMSO
Hey you guys way to go
I have a hunch

We're a talented bunch
What a show, what a show, what
a show

In memory of the formal dinner
An awesome experience for a
beginner
Such a feast
To say the least
It really was quite a winner

We've made it through our
classes
So, lift up your glasses
I just want to impart
From the bottom of my heart
I wish the best to the masses

To all our guests a toast

You're the best...the most
Thank you for being here
We'll give you a cheer

To all the guests who are here
It's so good to have you near
With support from you all
We stand straight and call
We will march forward despite
our fear

I can't think of better lands
Then a place called the
Netherlands
Our greetings we extend
To this country our friend
As we salute with both hands!

A toast to our speaker I recite
So, raise your glass up to the
light
Brigadier General W. Porter our
guest
Has come here from the
Midwest
So, we'll give the best from each
flight

Thank you for your speech
It really was a peach
Brigadier General Sir
Your words are worth more
than fur
Thanks again for your speech

A toast to the head table
A group who is very able
You are all very good
It is well understood
That you have really kept us
stable

Colonel Falconer please tell us
How is the food we selected for
mess?
We voted quite fairly
The minority won squarely
What's for desert, can you
guess?

Hail to the big #2
Vice Center Commander of
Sheppard, that's you
Colonel Carol I pray
You're enjoying your day?
This toast is solely for you

Amen to Major Jensen
Who teaches a great lesson
So now that we're blue
Amen to you...Amen, Amen,
Amen!

We jog and drink our milk
So, we need not the staff of Belk
But they are there
And they all care
So, cheers to Colonel Belk

Let's lift our glass to Colonel
Redding
His staff provides our bedding
I hear because Duffy's, we use
The latest of news
Is that someone planning a
wedding?

Cheers to Captain Hughes
Who taught us to wear blues
Her jokes were fine
So, lift your wine
And toast to Captain Hughes

Cheers to Major Keeling
He is quite appealing
In his Arkansas style
He lectured a while
And left us with good feeling

There once was a Major called
Pons
Who's named rhymed only with
bonds
She's worth quite a few
If you take stock in this view
Thanks for your help Major
Ponds

This one is for Randy and John
For making the time not as long
Your jokes were all great
Truly first rate
We will miss you both when
we're gone
To us- lift your glasses
We made it through our classes
We're ready to start
So, from deep in my heart
I wish the best to the masses!

Aim High!

I was proud to be in the Air Force Medical Corp! I was having a good time in MIMSO. I had my own definitions for the "Air Farce:"

Briefing- They line us up and flash their "Fruit of the Looms" at us.

Drill- When the flank stomps holes in the road and saves the construction engineers of the base the effort in their reconstruction roadwork.

And sayings:

In the Navy, we're all in the
same boat
In the Army, we're all in the
same tank
In the Air Force, we're all in the
same airplane!

I was so *fatigued* from marching
I turned Olive Green!

In the summer, everyone has the
right to bare arms!

We practiced marching in
flank at MIMSO. The platoon

leader was a short spunky woman who would say "Forward Harch" instead of "Forward March." She learned this in ROTC because it was clearer to hear or something. I could not get the proper women's shoes. They did not make my size. I wear fourteen and a half in women's shoes! I had to carry a note around with me. If I was stopped during inspection, I was to present the note which said I was wearing men's shoes because they did not make my size in women's shoes! Everything you wore in uniform had to be regulation. I joked...even the orange juice stain on the front of the uniform had to be two inches to the left of the third button! I was out of regulation because I was wearing men's shoes! Later this became an issue for the Air Force psychiatrist like it was some sexual identity thing!

I was ready to start the Nursing Internship Program after I graduated from MIMSO. I drove on my own from Sheppard Air Force Base in Texas to March Air Force Base in California. I drove 4-5 hours a day. I stopped to visit Darwin in Albuquerque where he was a professor. He had a house up in the hills away from town. There were some big boulders that looked like they had faces on them. I wrote this poem about them:

Crystal Rock Faces

Misty shore covered with crystal

rocks

Wet with waves from the ocean

Measuring time longer than

clocks

They are moving without

motion

Mother Earth has seen it all

begin

Watching all are faces in the
rock
Their silent spirit dwells within
They do not need to talk

Crystal creatures stacked in a
mound
Inhabiting their domain
They make no sound
The crystal rocks so quiet they
remain
Heidi Lobstein

It is interesting to note the
boulders with the faces that

inspired this poem were nowhere near the ocean! I remember Darwin and I went to some hot springs up in the Jemez Mountains after hiking. I remember a picture that he took of me sitting all natural like a nymph fairy creature sitting on top of a rock. I was beautiful, my long curly hair loose over my shoulders and down my back. Darwin had a thing about his potato chips. I ate his special Texas chips and he was mad. I should have asked! After visiting my big brother, I took a trip to Las Vegas to visit my cousins. I hadn't seen Aleena and the crew since I lived with them that summer after High School. Aleena at this point was divorced from Jack.

Aunt Heather had died from a brain tumor. Danny, who had worked as a pit boss at Caesars Palace, suddenly had disappeared one day...probably wearing cement slippers at the bottom of Lake Mead. It is a family mystery.

March Air Force Base

So, I really didn't pay attention to the time. I didn't realize I was due at a specific time at March Air Force Base. The time was on my orders but I really didn't pay attention to it. After 4-5 hours of driving I started to fall asleep at the wheel and would check into a hotel for the evening. So, it took me much longer than the time I had been allotted. I drove through the mountains into California in awe. Everything seemed so beautiful...different from the flat cornfields of Indiana. I arrived at March Air Force Base unaware that I was considered AWOL. When I checked into the Nursing office at the Hospital I was called into Colonel Lanton's office and given a lecture about how much trouble I was in being AWOL. I was shocked. I didn't mean to cause a problem. I wanted to learn and do a good job in the internship program. I felt embarrassed and was ashamed I made a bad first impression. I must make it up to them and prove to be an excellent nurse. They won't be sorry they accepted me into the Nurse Internship Program. I would show them I was worth their time. I stayed in a hotel in Riverside the first few nights. A newspaper and cup of coffee were left at my door every morning. I felt very adult. I put on my uniform and went over to the base getting appropriate paperwork filled out and such. I was assigned housing. It was an apartment complex outside the gates of March Air Force Base in Moreno Valley near the Circle K convenience store. I didn't know at the time that this was a bad neighborhood. Apparently, lots of drug deals near the Circle K. There was no security gate to get into the apartments. Anyone could walk in from the street. This is where they housed their single female officers. I was ecstatic being real grown up and having my own apartment!!! I didn't have to share the apartment with anyone!

There was a heated pool as well. I was so amazed to be swimming outside in the middle of January! I'm from the land of ice and snow. I was swimming outside in the middle of January!!! Steam was rising off the pool. There was a nip in the air but hey...it was January! I had just moved my belongings in last night from my car. Of course, my two-stuffed Avanti Lions had not arrived in the moving van yet. It was a partially furnished apartment. There was a bed and some drawers in my bedroom. There were table and chairs in the dining area. The carpet was blue-gray shag. I had been running around the base getting things ready to start the Internship Program on Monday. I came back to my apartment in the afternoon on Friday to relax and swim. I put on my Red, White and Blue flag speedo swim suit and my red flip flops took my Sylvester the cat towel and went downstairs to the pool to swim. I swam for about an hour back and forth enjoying the fact that this was the middle of January!

The Gang Rape

The pavement was cold on my feet as I walked over to put on my red flip-flops and wrap myself in my big fluffy Sylvester the cat towel. The air was smoggy. There were mountains close by but they hid in the thickened air. Wrapped in the towel I walked up the long staircase to my apartment. I was on the second floor. I stood in front of my apartment door. The door was ajar. Not open all the way but about a foot open like the wind had pushed it. I don't really know how it was opened. It was open. I walked in and everything went black. I think I remember a crack sound. I don't know if it was my skull cracking or if it was the sound of whatever hit me breaking. I don't know.

I came to in a pea soup fog. My body was being crushed under the weight of a very large man on top of me. I couldn't expand my lungs to breath yet I heard myself screaming in a distance. He smelled of old socks, sweat, alcohol and diesel grease. I recall his pockmarked face close to my face and his greasy dirty blond hair falling over one of his eyes. I felt ripping pain inside me like I was being torn apart. I felt pain in my legs, stabbing searing pain. I felt sharp pain in my hip. My right arm was extended above me and I couldn't move it. Pain...terror...I'm going to die...I'm going to die...I'm going to die. I heard two men on my left laughing but couldn't see them. I heard them yelling and their gravely voices, but I couldn't understand what they were saying. I felt unbearable penetrating pain and I passed out again. Everything went black.

The Battlefield

It was pitch black. I was alone. They were gone. I

couldn't move my head. My hair was stuck to the carpet with dried blood. My head hurt, everything hurt. My hip felt like it had been pulled out of the socket. My right hand was tied above me. I reached over with my left hand and worked out the knot in the dishtowel tied to the leg of the kitchen table and restraining my right hand. With both hands, I picked at the dried blood in my matted hair freeing it from the shag carpeting fibers. I was naked. My skin was wet and something felt slimy. Blood? Was I bleeding? My insides were coming out. Was I dying? My head was free. I turned on my side. I felt my bowels evacuating. I vomited. I was dizzy. My head felt like an ice pick was piercing through it. I lay there terrified. Were they coming back? I got up on my hands and knees. I slowly crawled toward a thin stream of light coming through the frosted glass of the bathroom window. I reached up and turned on the light.

I was covered in motor oil, feces, vomit and blood. There were bruises in the shape of handprints on my torso, shoulders and thighs. Cigarette burns looking like chicken pock like fluid filled vesicles on the tops of my feet and on my leg and buttocks. Agonizing pain encompassed every breath. I hung onto the sink and painstakingly stood up. The room was spinning. I looked in the mirror. I hardly recognized myself. My lip was cut. My hair was matted with motor oil and blood. I felt a drawing pulling feeling like my insides had been torn out. Blood motor oil and feces were running down my legs. My anus wasn't closing all the way and there were feces leaking out. I leaned over the sink and vomited again. What happened to me? What happened to me? Were they coming back? I was terrified. I hung onto the walls for stability and walked back across the battlefield to the front door. It was closed. I locked it and dead bolted it. They probably thought I was dead. They left me for dead. That's probably why they didn't come back. They probably thought I was dead. I stood looking at my red white and blue speedo swimsuit shredded in a corner like the conquered flag on the battlefield. I must clean this up. I went back to the bathroom. I showered and showered and cried and cried. I showered and scrubbed my body. I threw on some sweats and began to clean up the environment. I took Ajax and my Sylvester the Cat beach towel and tried frantically to scour the blood, feces, vomit and motor oil from the carpet. It took the blue gray color out of the carpet so that the carpet had white splotchy patches. I wandered around my apartment for a long time. This didn't happen to me. This didn't happen to me. I was shaking and I sought refuge in the closet in the bedroom. I slept intermittently through the weekend awakened by sharp pains and terror. I didn't answer the phone. I heard it ring several times. I was afraid to speak to anyone, especially my family. I stayed in the bedroom closet listening to the silence. I was afraid to move for a long time.

The sun was coming up on what must have been the third day. I came out of the closet and went into the kitchen. I saw on my answering machine it was Monday. I had multiple messages on the answering machine. I listened to my mom's messages. "Where are you? Why aren't you returning my calls? I'm worried about you." I couldn't call her back. I couldn't tell her anything about what I just went through. Neither of my parents would be able to handle this. I couldn't even articulate what just happened to me. I made a peanut butter sandwich and ate it. Then I got dressed in my uniform. I placed two sanitary napkins in my underwear because I was afraid I would leak vaginally or from my anus. I was fearful that I would smell bad. The uniform covered my arms with long sleeves. I went to March Air Force Base hospital to meet the other interns. Everything hurt me. It was hard to move. My head was throbbing, pulsating and the ice pick was still sticking through my head. I was present but not there.

The Air Force Nursing Internship Program

My memories of the Air Force internship program are foggy at best. It is amazing that I made it through and graduated. However, I wasn't functioning well. I was spaced out. I had difficulty focusing, retaining information and completing tasks. My internship was extended for six weeks and I changed preceptors. I did not graduate with the other nurse interns. There were four of us. Madeline who was hypercritical and to her everything added up to a big zero. The classes we had were taught by big zeros and were a waste of our time. She already had nursing experience and felt comfortable with her skills. This was just repetition to her. There was Darlene who I admired. She joined the Air Force to travel and see the world. She came from Bakersfield, California. Riverside, California or Moreno Valley, California were March Air Force Base was located was not that much of a change for her. To her everything was honking. He had a big honking nose or his wound was a big honking mess. Nora was very conservative and had a very positive attitude. She was cheerful and helpful. She stayed in the Air Force for quite some time after the initial obligation of two years. I believe she was stationed in Colorado. I recently friended her on Facebook. She still enjoys hiking and looks youthful and energetic. Our Internship Coordinator Captain Garcia was understanding and very nice. We all lived in the apartments that were across from March Air Force Base in Moreno Valley. This is where they housed single female officers. Captain Garcia made me feel welcome and she could see I was trying very hard to do well in the internship program.

They knew how to teach in the military. If I needed to learn how to put in an intravenous line, then I was sent to the operating room where I put in intravenous lines all day. By the end of the day I was an expert in putting in intravenous lines. By the end of the nursing internship program I was teaching the student nurses who came for their clinical experience how to put in an intravenous line! We also had the red flag field training during our internship program. We learned how to shoot an M-16 and practiced out triage scenario out in the desert. The sleeping bags were made from paper and we called them elephant Kotex! Most people disposed of their elephant Kotex after the training but I drew a Joker on it with markers and used it for a Halloween Costume at Edwards Air Force Base the following October. I went around saying, "I'm such a card!

I'm such a card! You'll have to excuse me. I'm not playing with a full deck tonight!" We ate MRE's meal rations during Red Flag training. As I remember the dehydrated nutrient dense cuisine was quite constipating. During Red Flag training, we slept in tents with wooden floors much like I did back in my Girl Scout camp days.

I remember there being a talent show at March Air Force Base. The winner of the talent show was reassigned to travel around entertaining active duty people in the USO Talent Show. There was a very good guitar player who played and sang and won first place. I did a three-skit solo mime show and won third place! I got the trophy that I had always wanted. I had never gotten one competing in the drama group or debate team in High School. I still have the trophy sitting high up on a shelf in my room today. The only trophy I have ever won! When I went to Edwards Air Force Base after the internship program I swam competitively and won a third-place bronze medal! So, I not only have a trophy, I have a medal as well! This means a lot to a high achiever. It is something tangible I can hold in my hand to show my success.

Two months into the
internship program we were
told Captain Garcia's apartment
was broken into. She had walked

in on the perpetrators after being away on a trip. She was beaten up and raped. I remember the look in her eye when she apologized to the nursing intern's that she would no longer be supervising us. I remember the look in her eyes. Why didn't I report the gang rape? Why didn't I protect Captain Garcia? It was my fault she was hurt. I did nothing to prevent these rapists from raping again. I felt, as my peers would have said, "like a big honking zero." I felt guilty. At that point I could not even articulate what I had been through. But I acted it out. I was very regressed and child-like. I was tap dancing down the stairs at the hospital and Colonel

171

Lanton told me I was "highly inappropriate Lieutenant!!!" I was the crazy woman. I felt I was going insane. I had great difficulty sleeping, I couldn't focus, and I couldn't retain information very easily. I went to Mental Health Services and while I was waiting to speak to a mental health practitioner I had a meltdown crying uncontrollably. I was told "This is not appropriate behavior for an Air Force Officer!" The psychologist there, Captain McDonald told Colonel Lanton that he could not do a psychiatric evaluation on me, as I was a "friend" of his from Red Flag training. The new supervisor of the interns, Captain Saffley and my friend

Darlene coaxed me with an invitation to my first "In and Out" burger and milk shake. I was stuffed with a burger and a shake and driven to a civilian hospital nearby. The next morning I was air-vacced by plane up to Travis Air Force Base for a psychiatric evaluation. I remember being given a Rorschach test. After I told him what I saw in the inkblots I turned the card over where there was writing in a rectangular box. I told the psychiatrist it looked like ants on a stick of chewing gum. He took the card away. I'm not sure what they were testing with that but it seemed to be a test for creativity. I was on the defense and trying very hard to prove I wasn't crazy. I passed the evaluation. I returned to March Air Force Base Hospital to continue the internship program. Each intern had to do a project that would somehow influence the environment of the hospital. Most of the other interns wrote up standardized care plans for care of patients with specific ailments. I painted a mural on rank which depicted team work in the Air Force. I was the bench, the butter bar or second lieutenant. Behind me was the first lieutenant, the back of the bench giving me back support. Against the tree were captain bars and up on the branches gold major leaves and silver lieutenant colonel leaves. Then a full bird colonel sitting up in the branches and another full-bird taking flight toward the one star general. All the green stripes or grass were the enlisted holding the dirt in place and preventing the erosion and the tree from toppling over. All this was painted using acrylics in bright color and childlike animation on plywood. This mural is portrayed on the cover of this book. I created it on the spot in my living room where I had been gang raped. After the mural, the blue-gray shag carpet was completely destroyed by the previous blotchy white patches and more recent paint stains. When I graduated the nursing internship program with all standards or above standard evaluations I donated this mural to the hospital to hang it up and people could be influenced by the big picture of how we all work together. They never hung it up. The excuse was that they were waiting for "funds" to hang it. How much do four nails cost?! When I left the Air Force I drove back to March Air Force Base to retrieve the mural from a closet and took it with me.

BEACON   Friday, September 11, 1987   Page 11

U.S. Air Force photo

Mural

2nd Lt. Heidi Lobstein touches up the mural she painted and donated to the hospital. "I wanted to share a part of myself with others," Lieutenant Lobstein. "The mural, under the guise of a management project, enabled me to do this. As a management project, I believe it succeeded. It will have a positive influence on the hospital."

177

Edwards Air Force Base

Originally assigned to Vandenberg Air Force Base I was rerouted to Edwards Air Force Base. I arrived at Edwards Air Force Base unaware that technically it was a remote site! I drove through the desert for a long time wondering where the gates of the base were. All I saw for miles was desert. I wondered, "Where did they send me?!" I drove and drove and drove...desert...desert...desert! When I finally arrived, I found that I would be living on the base in officer's quarters. I had a washer and dryer in my apartment which was cool but the carpeting was having a

schizophrenic episode and
needed to go back to the Las
Vegas casino from whence it
came!

Soon after my arrival I
joined the swim team. They had
a nice indoor pool. I preferred
swimming to running and
wanted to keep in shape. As I
mentioned in the last chapter I
came in third in competition and
won a bronze medal! I started
working at the hospital
supervised by a more
experienced nurse. Amy was my
preceptor. I was working
medical surgical nursing. I
remember we had a patient
come back from ICU and he fell
to the floor and turned blue.
Apparently, it was a pulmonary
embolism. My preceptor called a

code blue and everyone feverishly worked on him. All I could do was stand out of the way and say, "He's blue...He's blue...He's blue..." My preceptor finally sent me out to deal with his family. I was comfortable giving the family support and allowing them to hold my hand and cry on my shoulder. I had compassion and could connect with other's feelings. During an emergency, crisis and under pressure I shut down. I was dealing with routine and functioning with day-to-day activity of the medical surgical unit. But my heart was in working with the people and getting to know them. I didn't like to be in rush crisis mode. During our orientation, the counseling center introduced themselves and informed us that they were there for us active duty people. Free counseling. I thought it was a good idea. I had a lot of trouble sleeping and was easily distracted. I went in to get free counseling. I did not know there was no confidentiality at the counseling center. I mistakenly trusted the female counselor there. I disclosed a little family history and complained of trouble sleeping. She asked me if I had any old mental health records. I thought I could review them with her and she could help me sort things out and clarify what things meant. I needed validation. A month later I had just gotten back from a swim meet. I was in my new blue and white striped Speedo. There was a knock on the door and then in busted the military police! Apparently, the counseling center had told Colonel Sooner the commander of the hospital that I had gone over to the counseling center. Colonel Sooner did not know me. He ordered a psychiatric evaluation to be done. At the time, I did not know any of this. It had taken a month for the ball to get rolling. Apparently the old records I had given the counselor were a big red flag. The old records became an issue and the thinking was that this indicated that I had a "pre-existing" condition! At that point I was adjusting to the new base and had been functioning fairly normally at work. The military police forced me to put on hospital pajamas and restrained me to a stretcher. I had them take my backpack and uniform with me. I was air-vacced to Lettermen Army Hospital in the Presidio area of San Francisco with a room that looked out on the Golden Gate Bridge! When I was left in the waiting room at Lettermen Army Hospital I was in a confused state of mind. I was dissociating and wandered around the Hospital grounds until they came and escorted me to a locked psychiatric unit. I remember a male staff on the psychiatric unit saying to me as he went through my backpack and threw my neatly folded uniform on the floor in a heap, "Borderlines! I likes working with Borderlines!" I was there a week and totally regressed. I was pretending like a small child that I had a dog at the end of a stick that I had picked up on a walk through the Presidio area. This dog (stick) went around peeing on the doctor's legs. I remember a band of white lab coats asking me questions and all I could do was withdraw into my fantasy world and not look at them. At one point, they had me working with clay. I was cutting and pounding the clay to get the air bubbles out so when it was fired in the kiln it wouldn't break apart. I rolled the clay into long strips and cut the strips to make beads. The psychiatrist wrote that I was making penises and pounding on them for attention. He also wrote that I was out of regulation uniform wearing men's shoes. Like it was a sexual identity crisis and not just the fact that I had big feet!!! I used my creativity as an escape. I cut the thermometer covers that I had collected each time they checked my temperature to different lengths and made a pan type whistle out of them. At the end of the evaluation I was sent back to Edwards Air Force Base for discharge! They would not let me continue working the floor as a nurse. I was sent to the library where I was to type up cards. I was frustrated. I was not good with the secretarial skills. I broke down crying uncontrollably. Colonel Clay did not like me falling apart and gave me a direct order to "Stop Crying Lieutenant!" I looked up with tears streaming down my face and sobbed, "What if I can't?" "An article 15 Lieutenant! Do I make myself clear?" He threatened. All I knew was that an article 15 could land me in Leavenworth Prison. After a while they allowed me to teach a class I developed about addiction. I called the class "Crash and Burn" I got a good response from the Airmen who had a problem with drinking who were required to take it. I found that if I had gone to the counseling center for a drinking problem I would have been sent to rehabilitation. However, since I went in for help coping I was labeled "crazy woman" and kicked out of the Air Force! Drinking was an acceptable way of coping with stress. It was encouraged. "Go to the officer's club and have a drink!" If I had soused my problems with alcohol I may have gotten help! Now I was "crazy woman" being discharged for substandard performance of duty even though all my evaluations were standard or above! I was labeled with a personality disorder and discharged!

The Camping Trip

One of the men I dated in the Air Force took me on a camping trip. It was March and the weather in the San Bernardino Mountains was still unpredictable. When we started out Kevin took most my clothes out of my backpack and had me leave them in the car to lighten the load I would be carrying. I was left with basically a sweatshirt and some food. I was grateful for this because the trek was long and as we got to higher and higher elevation the air became thinner and it was harder to climb. We reached a beautiful clearing before dark and set up camp. Our tent was a simple tarp over a rope strung between two trees. We built a fire and had a warm meal. We enjoyed the moon and the stars and told a few ghost stories. There was another couple with us. The other couple had a state of the art tent. Soon the temperature began to drop. We turned in for the night and snuggled down into our sleeping bags. Then it began to rain! Our little lean-to was not holding up well and Kevin and I started to get wet. Kevin then told me to take off all my clothes so that we could use the body heat between us to keep us warm and alive. He rolled up his sleeping bag. His cold wet naked body crawled into my sleeping bag. We had to coordinate turning and breathing for the next eight hours. In the morning, I woke up to the ground covered with a white blanket of snow! It was so cold it had turned the rain into snow! I quickly got dressed. All I had was a thin sweatshirt. We packed up and started down the side of the mountain. I felt very sleepy. I wanted to lie down. I slowed down and c/o feeling tired. Then my vision started turning gray. The next thing I knew Kevin was facing me and screaming in my face...yet he sounded far away. "JUMP! JUMP! JUMP!" he yelled. I began to jump up and down. He got behind me continuing to yell physically pushed me to keep me moving forward down the trail. We reached the car and

Kevin turned on the heat. I looked in the mirror on the visor flap. My lips were blue and there was a white pallor around my mouth. As I warmed up Kevin told me that I could have died from hypothermia! He saved my life. Thank God, he had survival skills and knew what to do!

The Wait

I anticipated finding a nursing job after I was out of the Air Force and started to collect letters of recommendation from some of the people on the base that seemed to like me. I got a letter from the Captain for whom I taught the "Crash and Burn" addiction class. I got another letter from one of the charge nurses who got out before me and began working at the University of California Los Angeles Neuro-Psychiatric Institute (UCLA NPI). I applied to UCLA NPI as well. I remember going to an interview in front of a panel of staff members. I wore my Air Force blues. I think they were impressed. I got the position. It would be a long time before I was discharged. The Air Force had been paying me to live off base. At Edwards Air Force Base, I was living on the base. The paycheck was all in code so I didn't understand it. They held me on the base without pay for 8 months and took my paychecks until the debt that they had created was paid back! UCLA held my job for me for over 8 months! I lived on credit cards for a while. Kevin didn't think it was a good idea for me to be running up my credit cards to the max and not paying on them. He told me to give them to him. I did. Poverty

that I experienced became so
bad that I was going over to the
church to get soup cans so I
could eat! I would date different
men to get free meals both at the
Enlisted men's diner and the
Officer's club. I was seen eating
dinner with a redheaded
sergeant. This was a huge deal
as I was an officer and not
supposed to fraternize with
Enlisted! What were they going
to do? Kick me out? I was
threatened that if I didn't
behave myself then I would get
less than an honorable
discharge. Two of the men
whom I dated and had bought
me dinner figured I was the
desert. One was Kevin and the
other was his friend Steven. I
didn't say no. I just dissociated

and mentally left. They
continued to have sex with my
body but I was not present.
Another of the men, who I went
out with, Jim, tried to make
some moves on me but realized I
was not there and stopped. Jim
was not a rapist and became a
strong shoulder to cry on. I
became a joke with the two men
Kevin and Steven, who took
advantage of me because I was
"easy." They posted road signs
on my porch, "Men Working"
"Open for Business" and "Yield."
My parents visited me at the end
of that time. I lay around and
cried and cried. My parents
knew something was wrong but
didn't know what. They felt
helpless because they couldn't
get me out of the Air Force any

faster than the system was getting me out. My mother freaked out when she saw the last of the signs that was put on my front porch, "Open for Business." I told her I put it there because people would come and talk to me and I'd listen to their problems. I don't think my mom really believed me but I think she wanted to believe me. She didn't want to think about her daughter being raped. She probably was afraid I was being promiscuous but didn't know how to address that.

There was difference between the men who gang raped me. What they did was evil. The men in the two date rapes I experienced behaved in a very cruel way. I remember at the Officer's Club on Fourth of July these two men, Kevin and Steven, were "teasing" me and putting ice down my shirt to make my nipples show through my blouse. Kevin had bought my ticket for the BBQ and I was his date for that evening. I sought revenge on Kevin by putting ice down his pants. He was a tall strong man, the leader of the two, and he reacted in anger. He grabbed me by the neck and plunged my head down into the ice water in the ice chest, which held the beer and held me there. When I came up from the freezing water gasping for air Kevin and his sidekick friend Steven were laughing at me. "Oh...get over it!" "We were just

kidding!" I don't remember
exactly what happened after
that but Kevin took me to his
apartment after the BBQ before
the fireworks started and got me
into bed with him and raped me
from behind. I lost control of my
bladder and urinated on his bed.
Again, he became very angry
and hit me several times in the
face. I remember him saying to
me that I was "crazy" and no one
would believe me if I said
anything. He was an exemplary
career officer and certainly
outranked me. He smiled
broadly and said proudly that he
was an asshole. It was after this
incident when Kevin and his
friend Steven put the signs on
my porch. I felt like the local
whore. I could relate to the

Poncho Barns story. She used to be the madam of Edwards Air Force Base. She ran a brothel out in the desert. Every summer there would be a party out at the whorehouse ruins in the middle of the desert. After I had been out of the Air Force for a few months I came back in the summer for the Poncho Barnes party wearing Blue, Pink, Yellow and Green Neon Camouflage! It was camouflage for the city! I wanted to be seen and not be seen and to give the message that I was "fine." That what they did to me didn't hurt me. The reality is the culture of male comradery that condoned rape as a macho thing to do, damaged me. I've suffered for over thirty

years with depression and
mental health issues.

     While I was waiting to be
discharged I could leave base on
weekends. While I still had my
credit cards I filled up my gas
tank and spent the weekend in
Los Angeles visiting my cousins
from Russia. I swam in their
outdoor pool at a modest
looking apartment complex in
Culver City. Most of their friends
spoke Russian. They spoke
Russian to each other. Ivan was
in his 80's and was my mother's
father's brother. He was sweet
and hugged and kissed a lot. His
wife, Klara was much younger in
her 60's. She was his second
wife. Being with them gave me a
sense that I had a history and
belonged. I picked up a few

Russian words here and there. I liked to eat piroshki and borscht with sour cream with them. During the week, I sometimes would go with pilots to get their flying hours. They would fly small planes in and out of a very small airport in Kern County. I would go along to look out to make sure no other planes were taking off or landing, as there was no watchtower. I was towed up in a glider with one pilot and we rode the air currents to a safe landing. It was very quiet in a glider. No engine.

My friend Jim had an apartment full of guns and weapons. He also drank heavily. He has a heart of gold and is the kind of guy who would give you the shirt off his back. He would

come to visit me once I got out
of the Air Force and moved to
Santa Monica. We would eat
sushi together. Our legs were
the same length and we were
the same height so afterward we
would walk shoulder to
shoulder with coordinated steps
together traveling quite
efficiently and with speed. Social
life was good at Edwards and I
attended several parties with
Jim. You had to make your own
fun on a remote base in the
middle of the desert. One Air
Force officer had a "party
wagon" which was an old station
wagon type ambulance with
stickers all over it! It was the
hospital crew that served the
cheese dip in the bedpans, fruit
punch in the IV bags and

lemonade in the urinals! During one of these parties I left Jim downstairs and went upstairs and sat and talked with a female friend, Sarah, in the den. Later Sarah came downstairs and told Jim that I had been through some major trauma. I don't remember this but Jim recently reminded me of this incident. I told myself repeatedly that nothing happened. I was normal. I fought being discharged and went in front a panel of older men to prove to them that I wasn't crazy and should not be discharged. Of course, to them my dramatic flair and compassion just made me look crazy to them. Jim said that my style was Heidiesk. Over the years, he has always sent me birthday cards that were colorful and creative in a Heidiesque sort of way. I was surviving. There was a very caring group of individuals that gave me funds to move down to Los Angeles once I got out. They said just return the money once I was doing well so that they could help other military people in trouble. Things like having one's paycheck completely taken away must happen more than one would think to have a group formed to help others in distress! I did pay them back as soon as I started working at UCLA. It was quite some time before I was released. I got some advice from a JAG lawyer and did everything I could at first to stay and fight the discharge and then when that seemed impossible and I got the job at UCLA to hurry it up as much as possible. I wrote to my congressmen and a few weeks later I was called into Colonel Swift's office and told not to write any more lies to my congressmen. Again, I was threatened with an article 15. I was discharged within a week after that! I was discharged honorably but again with "substandard performance" and "character disorder." Hallelujah I was free. I drove to March Air Force Base and collected my Artwork. I was off to Santa Monica, CA where I rented a room in a house on Cloverfield with a bunch of young people.

Sweet Potato Jam

It was a Spanish style house with a tile roof. I had my own room. There was an older hippie like character who had come to California for primal therapy. He lived in the guesthouse in back and rented out the rooms in the house. His name was Avery. He had a psychotic dog named Chester. In the house was a very loud music playing red head named Tatum who worked as a drug counselor when she wasn't high on amphetamines! In the room, next to mine was Eve, a foreign exchange student from Germany who was studying psychology. I was focused on starting work at UCLA NPI. I worked on a Gero-Psychiatric unit with elderly patients. The unit was a nice cross between medical surgical nursing and psychiatry. There were two nurses that were getting ready to retire that took me under their wings and showed me the ropes. I worked on this unit for about 7 years. After 5 years, I became certified as a psychiatric nurse. I continued developing my teaching skills and put together a video with my friend Jim from the Air Force filming it and assisted by a friend of mine from the mime troop! The video is on psychological defense mechanisms. I called it "Immunology of the Mind!" I posted it on You-Tube recently and use it to teach my nursing students on how our psychological defense mechanisms work. Thirty years later. Same material. The video went from VHS to DVD to electronic to virtual!

I went for a long time working without a vacation. I decided to visit one of my coworkers who had worked as a traveling nurse at UCLA and then returned to her home in Hawaii. I didn't realize and I wasn't aware I was depressed. Suddenly, with the routine of work gone in one of the most beautiful places on this planet I stood on my friend's high balcony and instead of admiring the view all I could think about was jumping off and ending my life. How did I get there? It was like a dark cloud was hovering over my head even though I was surrounded by exquisite bio-life I could not enjoy it. I obviously didn't jump. What held me back was the same thing that kept me going. I felt responsible for others well being. What would that do to my friend if I jumped off while visiting her! What would that do to my mother? I hung in there. I had tried at one point to get help at the VA but was practically laughed out of the building. You're not a real veteran! You weren't in combat! You were only in 18 months! There was no women's clinic. Military Sexual Trauma was not recognized. I went to a private therapist, far away from UCLA. I didn't want to be fired for being crazy. In my mid to late 20's and early 30's I had several suicide attempts. I overdosed on pills and had to be revived. I was in and out of the hospital on 72-hour holds. Then the psychiatrist tried me on lithium at the suggestion of my therapist. While on lithium I maintained out of the hospital for a few years. Hence because I had stabilized on lithium I was labeled "Bipolar." My early years of therapy were about medication compliance. One of my first therapists was encouraging me to take Prozac. I made a necklace out of the pills and wore it to therapy. The therapist said that a lot of people who can't afford the medication would be grateful if they could have it. I was busy acting out my issues. I really wasn't ready to deal with anything. I moved from Cloverfield in Santa Monica with one of the roommates. Together we found an apartment in Pacific Palisades a few blocks from where we lived when I was born! I was in constant emotional upheaval and was not an easy person to live with I'm sure. I had poor boundaries. I remember eating some sweet potato jam from France that belonged to my roommate. My second vacation from UCLA was a trip to Europe. I looked all over France for that particular brand of sweet potato jam and could not find it. I brought back another brand of sweet potato jam but it wasn't good enough for this roommate. I traveled to France in search of a jam to absolve myself but to no avail! She was very angry when I gave her the different brand. I told her the other fell on the floor and broke. She didn't believe me. The three of us soon parted. I still worked at UCLA when I got a one-bedroom apartment on my own on Ocean Park Blvd. It was a single-story bungalow type apartment. I had wanted to be a part of a mime troop again. I even did some street mime on Venice Beach but I didn't know you needed a performing license. Two policemen stopped me and tried to get me to talk. I

took the right to remain
silent...mime code of ethics!
They started to handcuff me and
I broke down crying. A nice guy
who saw what was happening
asked them to please leave me
alone. They did take the cuffs off
and leave me but first warned
me not to be there again without
a license! I never did another
mime performance.

I took quite a few acting classes and did extra-work on movies and TV shows. I did a non-union Larry H. Parker commercial. I made $200 to lie. I'm not a good liar. I don't feel good if I lie, as I did about the sweet potato jam. It's unethical to lie. I had a moment of fame when I walked into Super-Cuts and the hairdresser there recognized me from the commercial!

In one of my acting classes we were going to make a movie on our own! I played the part of a sexy lawyer. They had to paint in cleavage! I also fell down roller-skating and skinned up both knees the day before they did a bunch of leg shots. They had to put heavy make-up on the scabs. We were making a go of it when one of the crewmembers stole all the expensive camera equipment! That was the end on my movie career!

I was in a stage performance of "It Had To Be

You." It was a two-hour play and only two people on stage. I did fine opening night, even though the character Theta Belau was much higher strung than I could ever be or portray. I had gotten off Prozac about a month before. I didn't expect what happened next. The day of the second performance I had a full-blown panic attack. I was so unable to function that I could not even open a box of cereal. I called an ambulance and the ambulance driver spoke to the director of the play and told him I couldn't make it. You know the show must go on attitude in show business...well it didn't. That was pretty much the end of my acting career!

And So, It Goes

Like my present therapist says,
"After you reach enlightenment
continue to chop wood and
carry water." Most of my life as a
nurse is routine. It's the unusual
incidents that stick out in the
mind. It gives me something to
write about anyway. I worked
on the Geriatric-psychiatric unit

until 1995. I think the worst thing that happened to me there was taking care of a patient with a colostomy bag and it splashed up in my face! There were a few challenges with Alzheimer's patients. One was "Sun-downing" quite severely. That means as the sun goes down in the evening the patient becomes very agitated and confused. I worked evening shift so when I came onto my shift at 3:30pm we would start medicating the demented patients so they wouldn't be out of control. There is only so much one can do. Sometimes the medication wasn't enough. I had one very strong male patient chase me around the unit. I ran into the nurse's station and slammed the door closed and locked it. His fist went through the glass window on the door. I called for a "staff assist" on the phone at the station. Other staff came to help and we safely deescalated the situation. I've had cups of water thrown at me when offering medication to the elderly but usually with the elderly population I wasn't at as much of a risk then if I was working with adolescence or adults.

I took some improvisation classes and comedy classes. I performed at Igby's and the Ice House as part of our class at "amateur night." I talked about working as a Geriatric-psychiatric nurse. I told the audience the "Rec Room" was the place where the patients "Wrecked the Room." It got so chaotic that I needed to go get the Ativan (tranquilizer). It took about five before I finally calmed down!!! It was dangerous on the unit! I got bitten by one of the Geriatric patient's once. I was walking around with dentures clasped onto my sleeve all shift!!! Timing is everything in comedy. Also, the audience makes a difference. When my audience wasn't responding, I would threaten to come out there and do Cardio-Pulmonary-Resuscitation (CPR) because the audience was dead. My timing was right on until I went into another depression and had the "S-L-O-W-S."

The unit secretary at UCLA took me under her wing and showed an interest in how I looked and presented myself. I always dressed down...slacks and a shirt. I was size 14 and slender at that time. We went shopping and I had a makeover. I came to work with my hair loose and a nice dress. Not practical but I definitely got noticed. One of the psychiatric residents asked me out.

Over the years, I dated a few men from the Sierra Club. The longest relationship was two months. I went out with a doctor named Ron Slaheel. It was right after a big Earthquake and the roads up North were closed to traffic in some places. We took our bicycles and did a several days trip. One night we slept under a picnic table. I woke up feeling hot breath on my face. Thinking it was Ron I opened my eyes and stared right into the eyes of a very curious cow! We fed it the broccoli that we had with us.

Ron and I even went to a nudist camp together. I loved swimming without a suit...very freeing. It seemed odd to see people naked at first, but after a while it normalized. We danced around the bon fire at night like a couple of heathens! The sensation of the wind on my skin was liberating. When we got ready to go home it felt weird to put on clothes again! I ended this relationship when Ron decided to travel on his own. I felt defective. Something was wrong with me. After I told one of the guys I was dating I had been raped he confirmed my belief and told me I was ruined. Toward the end of my employment at UCLA one of the men at work whom I became intimate with became demanding and wanted me to come see him when my parents were visiting me from Chicago. I reacted violently toward him out in the hallway at work and kicked him in the ass! I didn't connect the dots or understand why I was so angry. I was losing control of my emotions. One evening on the Geriatric-Psychiatric floor I called Marnie an asshole at work...everyone wanted to call Marnie an asshole. I just did. Instead of putting me out on medical leave at UCLA, they fired me. I was still working part time in an outpatient clinic at UCLA giving Risperidone injections. They didn't fire me from that UCLA job. The next day I was working with a Home Health Registry. I drove around Los Angeles using my Thomas Guide! We didn't have GPS! The person who oriented me was good at multitasking. She could drive a car while talking on a car phone (precursor to cell phones) putting on make- up, drinking coffee, smoking and orienting me to the paperwork!!! The paperwork had to be perfect for the insurance companies. If you made a mistake you had to copy the whole thing over. If your patients were far from each other and you had to recopy the paperwork often, this line of nursing was not very lucrative. Also, I got in a really bad habit of fast food stops when I was out and about. I began to gain weight.

The Fine Line

There was a fine line between being a psychiatric nurse and a psychiatric patient. I was both. I joked that I had earned my keys and worked my way up on the unit! Psychiatric units are notorious for multiple keys and locked doors. The unit that I had worked on at UCLA was a locked unit. I continued to go to therapy and take medication. I went to a bipolar support group on a regular basis. Initially I went to the support group at Step-Up on Second. I shared how I had been fired from the Geriatric-Psychiatric unit at UCLA and was working part time now in a clinic at UCLA and doing Home Healthcare. I was looking for something both more stable and more lucrative. One of the people in the group noted that they were asking for a Case Manager in the Partner's Program. I applied. This was a place where I could be very open about having a mental illness! It was to my credit and benefit that I suffered from a mental illness! I worked for the Partner's Program for two years. They didn't pay well but it was fun being out in the community with the patients. These were high utilizers and our mission was to keep them out of the hospital. I was young and would do things I would never do now. I drove a psychotic patient to his doctor to get an injection. He was seeing Jesus in the trees as I drove. Praise God he did not jump out of the car or something! I went searching under the Santa Monica pier trying to find one of my clients to bring her medication to her! There are things now that I just wouldn't do. However, I still go above and beyond.

At this point in my career I started on Risperidone. It seemed to slow me down and I could sleep better. I had frequent nightmares and headaches. On the Risperidone, I could focus better too. I had my first dog after I moved into a house on Jackson Ave. in Culver City. His name was Kadzak. He went to work with me sometimes.

The patients at Step-Up on Second
loved him.

I had a series of bad
roommates. One of the first ones
was a friend from Acting class,

Mitchel Barnipy. He was gay and proud of it! We had a mutual friend, Sunshine who was in acting class with us. We were all wannabees. Mitchel had boundary issues and taped a conversation between my mother and I. The conversation usually was my mom asking me questions and me baaing back at her avoidant of her finding too much about my life. We were close at a distance. One of the ways I remained close to my mom but not too close was to have her read to me on the phone. We went through the entire Harry Potter book on the phone over a time when it first came out. Well Mitchel was intrigued by the conversations I had with my mom and without my permission taped it and played it for Sunshine. I felt invaded. I was very angry. I told Mitchel to move out of my house. I came home to find that he packed a bunch of my belongings into his moving van with lame excuses, "You don't like that lamp anyway!" "You gave me the sweater!" We got into a full out brawl with the neighbors watching. I pulled off his toupee! Fortunately, nobody called the police. God had a better plan. I soon went to a better paying job working as a mental health worker at Twin Towers Correctional Facility. I had had a suicide attempt and while I was on a 1:1 with a psychiatric nurse she suggested I apply at the Department of

Mental Health on Vermont. When I went there one of the clerks came running out of her office. "I hear you are a mental health nurse!!! We need mental health nurses at the jail!" God put me in jail to work so I could listen to the inmates to see that I could easily be an inmate! I heard two inmates telling me how they got into a fight with their roommate or neighbor on the front lawn and were arrested! I was closer than I had imagined I ever would be to having a jail cell!

Jail House Rock!

I felt very needed listening to female inmates all day. They were depressed, lonely, isolated, mistrustful, battered, hurt, and abused. I spent my days listening to them. I got free food at the jail cooked by the inmates. Several times I was stopped by an inmate from eating something they made. They liked me. I was there for them. Hard telling what they might have put into it! I found grapes in the clam chowder once...I hope they were grapes. I had a habit that started back when I was doing Home Health Care stopping at fast food places. I would get three boxes of jalapeño poppers from Jack in The Box on my way home from work. I came early and left late using the desk and computer in my office to do my homework. I was working on my Masters in Nursing.

The psychiatrist I had added Depakote to the Risperdal. My Air Force weight was 155 lbs. I went from 175 lbs. to 245 lbs. in the years that I had free food at the jail and eating junk at fast food places on the way home. It was a free ticket to bad health. My parents and brothers were in shock that I had gained so much weight. My nerves were damaged too as I had hand tremors as a side effect from the medications. I had pre-diabetes and in my late thirties my period just stopped.

When I ballooned out like this I didn't want to be seen in public anymore. I stopped doing the stand-up comedy. I was doing sit-down tragedy instead. I didn't care. I sat and ate and studied. I got excellent grades in school; however, my lab tests were not passing. My glycosylated hemoglobin was over 7...I was facing being diabetic. I was diagnosed with a fatty liver. My theory on that is that the body is smart. The toxic crap from the medications I was on was wrapped in fat so the toxins wouldn't harm the body. I had never heard of detoxing at this point and had been heavily medicated for years. At one point I was on 17 different medications! I was taking antidepressants, mood stabilizers, neuroleptics, anti-glycosides, anti-acids, steroids, nebulizers, antihistamines, benzodiazepines...etc. I still had suicidal ideation and was given a handicapped plaque by my psychiatrist so I wouldn't have to park on the roof at the jail but could park downstairs. I kept thinking of jumping off the garage roof. There was even a set of steps by the wall on the roof. A movable set of steps. I kept imagining I would climb up the steps and just fall over the edge of the roof to my death. Then I really got freaked out. One of my coworkers committed suicide. I came to work one day and was told Karan had shot herself in the head! We frequently ate lunch together. She was always very upbeat and friendly. It was a shock. I thought it could have been me. Why her? Her funeral was the first funeral that I ever attended. She had a white coffin. There were lots of people at her funeral. It made me think of how a suicide affects so many people. I hung onto one of my coworkers and we cried and cried together. After that back at work nobody talked about Karan. It was the pink elephant in the room. We were psychiatric professionals unable to process what just happened.

Working at the women's jail opened my eyes to a whole

different side of life. Initially I was shocked. I was walking down a long hallway with female inmates lined up against the wall. The female deputy told them all to face the wall, drop their pants and bend over and cough. How humiliating. As a mental health worker, I listened to the traumatic impact searches had on inmates. I developed rapport with some of the inmates who were seen by mental health. I was by myself one Saturday covering Tower Two of the Twin Towers Correctional Facility. I got a panicked call from a deputy. One of the inmates had soaped up her body in the shower and was standing on the tier threatening to jump and because she was slippery from the soap nobody could hang onto her. If you ask me, it is a dumb design to have an open second level balcony in mental health where people could jump off. I rushed up to the pod were the inmate was. They had spread mattresses on the floor below to lessen the impact of her fall if the inmate decided to jump. I recognized the inmate. It was Litria who was an inmate who I had been seeing on a regular basis and with whom I already had some rapport. I told her I was just coming up to her to keep her company and I wasn't going to try to talk her down. She agreed to my presence. I spent two hours up on the tier with her. At one point the other inmates were yelling, "JUMP JUMP JUMP!!!" She leaned forward and I said, "You don't have to prove anything to them. How is your baby daughter? Did she visit with your boyfriend Sunday? She leaned back again and told me how much she missed her baby and feared that if convicted she would miss her baby's second birthday. Eventually Litria got cold and climbed off the railing and decided not to jump. She was put into one of the potholder material dresses with no sleeves and no underwear on and locked down in her cell. That situation had my adrenalin going. Even though their underwear and clothes are taken away some inmates find a way to harm or kill themselves.

One woman tore strips off the mattress to make a noose. So, her mattress was taken away and she had to sleep on the bare metal shelf. Another inmate took out from her mouth a denture plate that had a sharp edge on it and she cut up her arm with it. Yet a third inmate hung herself with her own hair extensions.

Despite feeling needed by the inmates, I was getting pressure from management. It was a different manager than the one who hired me. I worked with psychologists. The previous manager thought it a good idea to hire mental health nurses because we could also address the physical issues in addition to the psychological issues. Someone might be confused and a nurse would check the blood sugar to make sure it wasn't too low or assess for another physical reason before concluding the person was psychotic. Initially I was appreciated for being a nurse. With the new manager, I was asked to act like a psychologist or psychiatrist. I was told that I had to diagnose people using the DSM IV. This was beyond the scope of practice as an RN and I began to put my feelers out for another position. I had worked at the jail from around 1997-2004...about 7 years. I had the 7-year itch and I didn't want to lose my license. Brotman Hospital in Culver City was wining and dining me to go work there. It was two blocks from my house on Jackson and I walked to work! I just graduated with a Master's degree in Nursing Administration and Education. Brotman did not pay me for having the Master's degree. My parents were very proud of me getting my Master's degree and both were at my graduation ceremony.

If You Don't Like It Here...

Most of my friends I hung out with were from the bipolar support group I went to on Grosvenor Ave. in a place called SHARE. The facilitator of the group, Diane and her bipolar boyfriend, Hubert were friends of mine. Diane and I ate lunch together a lot. I was fascinated by the way she said eggs. She pronounced it Aygz. She told me of her life with Hubert. He tended to be verbally abusive. Nothing I would have tolerated. Hubert ended up on the psychiatric unit where I worked. I was put on a different unit until he left. It would have been a real boundary problem. Once he saw me when he was off the unit for a cigarette break and came running over, "THIS IS MY FRIEND HEIDI.... SHE IS GOING TO BUY ME MORE CIGARETTS!!!" I was pleasant but firm, "I can't do that Hubert. If you want I can call Diane and she can bring you some."

We were grossly understaffed at Brotman. They had the nurses spread thin and running. I requested more staff frequently and the response I usually got from the nurse manager was, "If you don't like it here, you don't have to work here!" Sure-enough on one of those days I requested more staff my psychiatric technician out on the floor was wacked over the head with a wet floor sign and needed stiches. There wasn't enough staff to control the patients. We needed more staff. People were getting hurt.

We had all kinds of crazy pressure. The 15-minute break was cut down to 10 minutes. I almost choked on my scrambled eggs one morning! To stay awake and alert I drank large 64 oz. cups of Coke a Cola. I was the unhealthiest I had ever been. I was hospitalized twice for severe asthma. My weight was at least 245 lbs. and I was swollen and bloated and toxic. While changing my psychiatric medication around my feet and legs became like elephant limbs. One of my friends from the bipolar support group named

Ona, used to come over and peel me off the couch and have me walk with her up and down on Venice Beach. I had gotten a Mickey Mouse tattoo and multiple piercings.

RAPE:
(A word is worth a thousand pictures)

Back when I was still working at the jail I continued to attend the bipolar support group meetings at SHARE. One of the meetings a man named Ted came and said he suffered from Attention Deficit Disorder (ADHD) and was looking for a group. I talked during that group about not feeling normal. I felt that something was wrong with me, as I didn't have a boyfriend. Afterward Ted came up to me and told me how wonderful I was and invited me for dinner on his boat. I had to leave my car several blocks away from the Marina to find parking and then got into Ted's car to go to the boat. It was a small boat but had a kitchen and bedroom downstairs. Once out to sea Ted made spaghetti for dinner. I didn't realize that I was the desert. After we ate I asked to go back to shore and take a walk around the marina. Ted inappropriately touched my crotch and said, "You feel that, don't you? You are normal." I froze. I didn't know what to do. There was nowhere I could go. Ted said he loved me and began to pull of my clothes. I even had a sanitary napkin on. It was toward the end of my period. He was touching me in my private area and when I pulled away he grabbed me and pulled me onto the bed. "You want to be normal and have sex don't you. Just relax." I thought maybe something was wrong with me and I didn't fight. Ona told me all about her sexual encounters with men and she seemed to really enjoy them. What was my problem? He penetrated me. It hurt. He was aggressively going in and out then he flipped me over and went into my anus. My head was up against the wall and he banged my face into the wall repeatedly. Then he was done. Was this sex? Is this what

Ona enjoyed so much? Ted drove me back to my car and followed me home. He talked about traveling around the world with me in his boat. He came inside. He had sex with me again, while on looked my dog Kadzak.

I walked around for three days going to work zoned out. When my Mom called, me she picked up that I sounded strange. I told her I was in love with Ted and that he wanted to be with me the rest of my life. I told her we had sex on his boat. She told me it was a rape and wanted me to go to the Emergency Room. This was three days later. They sent in a big male police officer in the ER and I completely shut down. I wouldn't even give them Ted's name. The next morning Ted met me at the i-Hop. He wanted to show me something in his car. I wouldn't go. When he asked why I said very audibly, "You raped me." He shushed me, "People will hear!" He equivocated. I said louder, "**You Raped Me**." That was the last I saw of him. When I went to visit my parents in Chicago my Mom had me take a mikvah bath. It's a ritual bath for cleansing where I had to take everything off...including all my piercings. The female Rabbi said prayers over me and submerged me in the water. It probably helped my Mom feel better. This was the first time in years that I had my earrings out and black stuff was coming out of the piercing holes!!! It really grossed out Harold!

Heidi's Hair Salon, "Curl Up and Dye!"

Back when I was going to Purdue University, or as my brother Darwin who also studied there called it "Undue Perversity," I had a roommate who told me that any time I was in trouble or having a difficult time I could pray using the name Jesus Christ and things would change. It wasn't until I was experiencing severe depressions and thinking about committing suicide in my late 20's and early 30's that I gave praying using the name of Jesus Christ a try. I had been depressed and had a dark cloud hanging over me for a few months. I prayed asking Jesus Christ to take away the depression. Soon after praying the dark cloud receded. The depression lifted and life was better! Through contact with my ex-roommate back in Indiana I found Jews for Jesus in Los Angeles. It was a small congregation lead by a family who home schooled their five children. I had fun with the kids. I use to do turtle impressions for the oldest girl who was around 11 years old. I bought the kids a jungle gym swing set equipment contraption so they could climb and have fun on their recess break. The youngest girl age 2 used to come to church with her pretty dress on but take off her diapers in the middle of everything and run around bare butt! "Freedom! Freedom!" Kind of like my first dog Kadzak running down the street after breaking out of the yard. "Freedom! Freedom!" It is this reckless spirit of no confinement for which we all yearn.

I was still working at UCLA and had just discovered Jesus when I went with a coworker to her Apostolic church and became filled with the holy spirit and by the end of the service put on a jump suit and got dunked in the "mikvah" to get baptized. It was the first time I heard people speaking in tongues. Much later at Brotman

Medical Center I befriended a nurse who was a pastor as well. I would wake up at 4 am and go over the hill to Lamert Park and pray in tongues at 5 am in the church she belonged to. I was more comfortable praying in tongues than in English. I didn't have to think about what to say and I would just naturally flow with a language that sounded like it came from Mesopotamia B.C. E. I felt special being the only Jew there. The pastor there gave me a feeling that I was very blessed and was chosen to be an instrument of God. I learned that Jesus came through the line of King David. Also, when the temple was destroyed by the Romans in 70 A.C.E. the sacrificing animals stopped. I took that to mean we didn't need to sacrifice animals anymore. Jesus was the sacrificial lamb. I think he is an example of how we can model our behavior after him and how to act toward each other. Some of my friends would laugh and say I'm a confused Jew. I don't think so. I'm first and foremost a humanitarian. So was Jesus. He has love in his heart for human kind. I have compassion. I'm an empath. I try to see through the eyes of whomever I'm trying to help.

When I was working at Brotman there was a young woman I had as a patient who was blind. When I was walking with her I learned to knock on doorframes and walls so she could hear where she was in relationship to them and could use auditory input to guide her. I liked the way she asked for footies or slippers. She called them "foogies." Unfortunately, she was blinded and became brain damaged from multiple beatings from her boyfriend. I connected to her and brought her some clothes to wear that had raised letters on them so that she would get tactile input and she could differentiate her outfits. The next day I came in to work and the housekeeper was wearing the shirt that I had given the patient!!! I confronted her on stealing from a patient and she denied that she had stolen it and said that the patient had given it to her! The blind woman was now carrying all her clothes around with her in a pillowcase! She knew someone had taken something from her. Maybe the housekeepers were on furlough from Twin Towers Correctional Facility? I could not make much headway getting her shirt back for her.

I had an elderly woman choke to death on mashed potatoes when I worked at Brotman. I couldn't get the airway open because the mashed potatoes stuck in her windpipe. You don't see too much death and dying when working on a psychiatric unit, however, it does happen. When it does it is a shock. We weren't sure what to do with the body.

The morgue staff didn't pick it up for a long time. We kept the body covered with a sheet in the dining room for hours until they came. Of course, the other patients are all upset and want to look. One of my coworkers got the "hebe-jeebies" as she helped me cover the body with the sheet. She didn't want to look at the deceased. She was a real pretty nurse that wore lots of make-up and had multiple highlights in her hair. She didn't want to get her hands dirty.

There was another death of one of the patients at Brotman I remember. A new patient came in with a diagnosis of Chronic Obstructive Airway Disease (COPD). She arrived at the end of my shift so I endorsed her admission to the next shift. Apparently, they didn't make an assessment but just gave her sleeping pills, which made her respirations slow down even more. I came in the next morning and they had been marking her down on the rounds board as sleeping. I went into her room to wake her up for breakfast and she was stiff and cold. She had died sometime during the night. I was told to start Cardio Pulmonary Resuscitation (CPR). On a dead person! We did a full code attempting to revive her until the doctor came and pronounced her dead. Everyone was pointing fingers at each other. Oh no, she was fine last night...it just happened! They even tried to pin it on me as if I neglected to do the admission; except I documented that I endorsed the admission to the night shift! One thing I learned in nursing. You must document everything to cover yourself. If you don't document, it then it didn't happen.

My dad had a heart attack February 14, 2005 when I was still working at Brotman. He had 5 stents put in and was put on Lovenox to prevent blood clots. The last time I saw him was in the Spring around Passover 2005. This was the first time he ever looked frail and elderly to me. I bought a bigger house in Mar Vista in 2004 with plans that my parents would move back out to California and I would take care of them in their old age. My dad never made it to my new house. He fell and hit his head on the bar inside of a fold out couch he was trying to open. He bled out in the brain. My mom and I were arranging rehab when he started to recover. Then he had a massive stroke on the other side of his brain. He died October 22, 2005 but they unplugged the ventilator October 25, 2005. The luggage tags and airline tickets to come to California were on his desk.

Answer My Question; I'll Question Your Answer

We didn't have a funeral. My mom had my dad cremated so she could take him out to California with her. It was the most economical thing to do. She wanted to save his ashes and be cremated as well when the time came. She wanted her ashes mixed with his ashes and together scattered over the Pacific Ocean. How romantic is that! My mom told me that the rabbis did not support her in this decision. They had reservations about cremation because of all the Jews in the Holocaust who were burned and cremated. The rabbis didn't come to my mom sitting Shiva for my dad. At a time when she needed support! My mom described feeling like a torn piece of cloth, never to be whole again. After 53 years of marriage, I don't wonder. When people are together that long they even start to look alike. My mom and dad had complimentary haircuts. My dad was bald on top and had a gray horseshoe around the sides and back of his head. My mom had gray hair on top but had the sides and back of her head extremely short. It was like her hairdresser put a bowel on her head and trimmed and shaved everything below the bowl line. They had traveled quite a bit together during their retirement. During the 7 years when Harold wasn't speaking to my parents they were traveling to Israel and visited the Wailing Wall. My mom wrote a prayer that her son would communicate to them again. As soon as they got back home Harold called them to find out how they were doing!!! Power of prayer! Now when my mom lost her husband and then had to move out of the Town Home they rented because the owner was going to knock them down and build Condos, Harold was concerned that she would move in with him. He told her she couldn't move in with him and his wife. I went back home about 6 months after my father died. My mom was wandering around the Town Home like a lost lamb. She was the only one in the complex. Everyone had already moved out. I started to pack up her things. I had refinanced and used the money to remodel the back room, put a bathroom in and install central heating and air conditioning. My place was ready for her. Harold's wife Benita traveled with my mom after they had everything packed up and moved out to me. They came with my dad's ashes. Everything was moved from my parent's house into mine. The previously mentioned easel which my mom would not destroy despite the opportunity to do so, my dad's Bertoia chair with his blood stains on it from having thin skin and being on anticoagulants, his toothbrush and even a year-old box of petrified chocolates in the shape of a heart. I took time off from Brotman and helped my mom get oriented. Love is a baffling concept. Despite saying she wanted to divorce my dad, my mom loved him very much. I loved my mom intensely too. I had similar energy to my dad as we were both being Aries type people. I think she improved being around me although it completely up rooted her. I can't really define what love is. It's not just a feeling. It is an energy that is defining. Intense love signifies who we are in relation to another. When we lose that other relationship, it hurts. We

loved them. The love was a part
of us almost like an arm or a leg.
Losing someone is like an
amputation of a part of us. What
is love? Answer my question and
I'll question your answer. Love
is elusive yet so obvious.

Come Get Your Mother!

I didn't go back to Brotworst (Brotman). After being a unit representative and helping to negotiate the nurse's contract I continued to be frustrated trying to change things for the better and meeting resistance. "If you don't like it here," mentality got to me and I looked elsewhere. Several Brotman employees had jumped ship and gone to the Veteran's Administration. I put in an application and 8 months later I was called to start working on 2 South AB psychiatric unit. My dad would have been proud. They paid me for having my Master's degree in nursing and I got a bump up the pay scale for being a veteran!!! I was proud to serve those who served again. I settled into the routine of working an 8-hour evening shift after a chaotic orientation. The charge nurse who already had a full plate was supposed to orient me. The unit couldn't hang on to a nurse manager for more than a year and there were some real funky politics around there. I found exposure to the floor wax stripper that was named "Excessive Force" almost killed me. In an enclosed space with very little ventilation breathing that stuff in I had a major asthma attack. My pulse oxygenation went down to around 80%! I was hospitalized at Brotman and my mom stayed with me in the room. They skipped a treatment at night. My mom was asleep. I literally crawled to the nurse's station to get them to give me a nebulizer treatment. I couldn't even eat because chewing and swallowing took away from the effort I needed to breath. I notice when my oxygen gets low like that I get rather punchy. I could do wheel-chair comedy instead of stand-up comedy! From then on if they had to wax the floors at the VA I had to leave. One time the charge nurse told me to wait outside until the fumes cleared. She said she would call me on my cell phone when housekeeping left and the smell dissipated. It took several hours. I got the roller-skates from my car and roller-skated around the VA hospital. That was a mistake. I was seen roller-skating around the hospital! How inappropriate lieutenant! I felt like I was back in the Air Force. They made a big deal out of it. The charge nurse probably should have sent me to work on another unit until the air was clear. That situation was just silly. Any way it affected the way management viewed me. I got off on the wrong foot with the nurse manager on 2 West AB. I was wearing fatigue-patterned scrubs. She told me that this pattern could trigger PTSD in the patients. I laughed and asked, "Where is the research on this?" After all they were always screaming evidence-based practice!!! She didn't like me after that. I don't think she liked very many people. She had "Nurse Control" on her door. What a power tripper! You don't control nurses. You command nurses leading people in the direction you want them to go. I interviewed for a nurse manager position on 2 South AB multiple times but I was not politically correct!

Several times as I was working in the evening I would get calls from people on my cell phone. "Hello...I'm calling about your mother. She is here. I have her here in the Hinano Cafe on Venice Beach. She was wandering around lost and had me call you on her cell phone. Can you come get her?" I left work and was on my way. One

time she was lost by Helms
Bakery and managed to call me
on the cell phone herself. She
had gotten off the bus too soon.
Initially my mom had gotten
better when she moved in with
me. I would come home after
work and we would watch the
late late late show and eat
chocolate and cookies she had
hidden around the room. My
mom's experience paralleled the
times when she used to wait up
for her dad coming home from
work late at night. Her
experience also was reflective of
being at the boarding houses in
Belmar, New Jersey where Aunt
Jenine had renters. I rented out
my extra rooms to a massage
therapist with a young daughter.
My mom use to give his

daughter art lessons and be a
grandma figure she hadn't had.
And the little girl was a
granddaughter figure for the
granddaughter she didn't have.

One evening I came home
from work and my mom was
down on the floor near her
closet. She hadn't fallen but had
gotten down looking for
something and could not get
back up! I couldn't lift her either.
I got down on my hands and
knees in front of her and she
used me to stabilize and push
herself back up. She had been
down on the floor for hours
before and hadn't been able to
find anything to hold onto to
push herself up. My mom use to
jog and keep in shape with
Darwin's influence. She was

losing strength and her memory was becoming more impaired. She had bouts of confusion one in which she asked me if I was her daughter! At times, she got on my nerves because it sounded like she was criticizing me. I suddenly jumped up after she said something, which I interpreted, as I wasn't good enough or doing enough and started hitting myself in the face. I ran down the street and onto the freeway crying. I was thinking of throwing myself in front of a car. The police picked me up and drove me to the police station. I was talking in tongues and very agitated. From there I was placed on a 5150 and driven to College Hospital for a psychiatric admission. My mom was so upset by my reaction that she went to her friend's house up in the Pacific Palisades where we used to live and spent the night. I think things settled down between us after that. She wasn't so critical and I wasn't so reactive. My mom wanted me to marry a "Nice Jewish Boy." I told her not to sweat it. I was going to marry a black lesbian from Pluto. We always had this kind of psychological warfare between us. Back when I was going to Purdue some of the mimes invited me to go to Florida with them on Spring break. My mom literally said, "Over my dead body!" I went home to Chicago instead. I sat under the reading light in my bikini and told my mom I was pretending to be in Florida. She came and poured a glass of water over my head and yelled, "WAVE!" It was, as I said, psychological warfare. Who could play the game the best?

The three years that my mom came to live with me were critical in my growth. I became the caretaker and my mom became childlike. She came into my room frightened like a small child when my roommate was drunk and had his music blasting at 2 am. I comforted her, provided for her, and took care of her. When my roommate lost his iguana, I looked in my mom's room. I knew it would freak her out if she found it. With her reptile phobia, it might send her blood pressure too high and she might have a stroke. I was very concerned about my mom's blood pressure. It was running high. I thought I would lose her from a stroke. I took her to my doctor and put her on blood pressure medication. Her pressure was still high despite this. I took her to an acupuncturist who diagnosed her with "liver-fire." The acupuncturist gave me some herbs to make into a tea. The tea was very bitter. My mom would not tolerate the bitterness. She had a sweet tooth. She consumed a lot of sugar. I didn't realize this at the time but since I have learned about Asian medicine from Darwin, my mom was feeding the cancer with sugar. My mom and I did trips to Sea World and Disneyland. We had a good time together. She was feisty though. At the end of the day walking with her arthritic knees all around Disneyland she was moving very slowly. One of the cast members came up to us with a wheel chair. My mom waved it away and exclaimed, "Get that thing away from me!" A week before my mom passed she took off her wedding ring, gave it to me and told me she didn't want just anyone taking this off her. I thought that was odd. Neither of us had any clue that she had anything wrong with her. On that Friday, my mom complained of a stomachache. I took her to the ER where they did some blood tests and told us her liver enzymes were all out of whack. She didn't want to stay in the hospital and came home over the weekend. At this time, Darwin had finished Asian Medical School and was moving in with me to help me take care of our mom. We were both close to my mom. Over the weekend my mom got weaker and stopped eating. I think the last thing she ate was a hard-boiled egg. Monday I brought her back to Brotman Hospital. They admitted her. Darwin took my hand and held it over my mom's head. I felt waves of energy coming from her head. Her *yang* was separating from her *yin*. "She's dying." Darwin told me.

My brother Darwin and I took off to Santa Cruz. My brother had been living up in the Los Gatos Mountains in a cabin. I had been there visiting the year before with my mom. I was going to leave my mom there and go to a nursing conference in San Francisco. However, the roads were so narrow going up and down the mountain I only wanted to make one trip. I didn't think my mom would survive in the mountain by herself either. It got very cold and I had to chop wood and light the old fashioned potbelly stove to heat up the house at night. Darwin didn't get back until very late. My mom and I just took a week to relax. I watched banana slugs slime across the grass and my mom painted in watercolor.

Darwin and I moved everything he had in one big truck. We were back on our way Thursday evening when we received a call from the doctor. My mom was diagnosed with 4th stage liver cancer and was being discharged to hospice care Friday. I insisted we have hospice care at home. I wasn't going to send my mom to a nursing home. My mom was alert and aware when she arrived home on Friday. One of the last things she said to me before she slipped into a coma was, "Who is going to take care of you?" I reassured her Darwin was here now and we would take care of each other.

The hospice nurses showed me how to give my mom the morphine under her tongue. I finally understood the very strange dream I had been having for years. I dreamed I was tangled up in IV tubing and Darwin came to help me get untangled. Well here was Darwin helping me with hospice care for my mom. That weekend they couldn't send any nurses from hospice so I ended up doing the physical care. Once I turned her and coffee ground emesis came out of her mouth. I cleaned her up and tried to make her as comfortable as I could. She was heavy to move as her abdomen and lower extremities were edematous. I didn't want to have Darwin help me because I didn't want him to have those images in his head. She had had an IV initially but toward the end she only had on oxygen as her organs were shutting down. It was bizarre that my roommate was making out in the kitchen on the other side of the wall with his German girlfriend. EXCUSE ME BUT MY MOTHER IS DYING HERE!

My mom had Cheyne-stokes respirations grunting and irregularly breathing. It was hard to tell if she felt pain...was I giving enough morphine? I played some music for her. She liked classical. The oxygen machine made a lot of noise. Darwin and I took turns at her side. Tuesday around 2 am Darwin woke me up. "I think

she's going to go soon," he said.
He went to sleep and I took over.
I turned off the oxygen. I told
her to go to the light. Her body
went from feverishly hot and got
cold starting from the
extremities. Her head was the
last of her to get cold. Her
respirations got less and less. I
cried and cried. I told her how
much I loved her. I felt her
presence in the room but her
body was cold and her
expression peaceful. No more
pain or struggling with
breathing. Toward the light
mom...toward the light.

I called the Neptune Society
and a white station wagon came
around 4 am. They had me step
outside the room while they put
her in a bag and wheeled out her

body. We had her cremated. I thought there was going to be a special service to bring her ashes back home but they sent them through the regular mail! My brother was stretching in the front yard after jogging and the mailman gave him a heavy box. Mom's ashes were inside. That's bizarre! How many people's ashes are shipped through the mail every day??? Special delivery…here is your mom!!! We put her ashes up on the bookcase next to my dad's ashes and surrounded them with pictures of the two of them. We still haven't gotten around to scattering their ashes over the Pacific Ocean. Maybe by the time this book gets published we will have done this. Darwin and I are waiting for Harold and Benita to come out from Chicago for memorial ceremony. Or maybe we will just wait until the whole family goes and the last one standing dumps everyone else overboard!

Time and Money

It seems to me that one measures time passing in relationship to significant other's passing. After my mom died Darwin and I became close. Darwin decided to stay with me and my roommate decided to move out to be with his German girlfriend. I think the loss was hard on his little girl. She lost her "grandma," art teacher and role model. For me this was a double loss of income. My mom was no longer helping with my mortgage and buying some of the groceries. My roommate left and Darwin did not want any more strangers running through the house. I had people sleeping on the couch and in the garage. It was becoming like a haven for those in need. It just happened that way because I had a lot of compassion and didn't say no. Even the cats in the neighborhood hung out at my house. I came home from work one day and my cat Schmoopy was surrounded by the neighborhood cat harem on my bed. They looked at me when I entered the room like I was intruding on them. "MEW! WHO ARE YOU? MEW!" Some of the people that had been my roommates were incredibly challenging. I had one that was pissed off that I asked him to move out and dumped cement down my bathroom sink drain. We have difficulty with the plumbing to this day. Darwin just didn't like the idea of having other people around. He tolerated my cat Schmoopy and my dog Sade. With the changing energy of the household the cats dissipated too. There were a lot of cats in the neighborhood then one day they all but a few old and scraggly looking cats were left. Schmoopy, being the scraggle-puss that he was, remained.

Schmoopy

Sade was a black Labrador.
She was nervous nilly and very
silly. Running and then stopping
to look at you with her head
cocked to the side and her paw
in the air and her tongue
hanging out. Kadzak had died
my first year on McLaughlin. He
had a tumor in his right front
leg. They removed the leg. He
still ran around on three legs. I
told Sade that is what happens

to bad doggies that run away.
We cut off their legs! My friend
Celia was horrified I told my dog
Sade that. "You'll make her
more neurotic!" She scolded.
Kadzak's cancer came back after
a few years. Kadzak and Sade
shared the dog run in back. The
flies knew Kadzak was dying
from cancer. The flies literally
ate off his ears until there were
two bloody stumps. I tried Tea
Tree oil and all kinds to
remedies to get rid of them but
nothing worked. Kadzak was so
weak he couldn't stand up
anymore. I took him out for a
McDonald's hamburger, which
he gobbled up and then I took
him to the veterinarian and had
him put down. Sade literally
went crazy by herself in the dog

run and dug under the fence and
burst through my screen door.
Ever since then she sat on a dog
bed pillow in my room by my
bed. She always had a
nervous/sad look in her eyes
like she just wanted more love
than you could give her.

Basically, my salary wasn't
enough to cover the mortgage.
Darwin with good intention
tried to develop our business
but it never became lucrative.
We help people with their health
issues at our house every
Wednesday night at 7:30 in our
free community clinic. We
hoped to funnel people into
using products as they need
them and that we use ourselves.
There are LifeWave patches,
which have crystals in them that

melt with body heat and send
out a frequency communicating
through acupuncture meridians
to enhance certain functions
that the body already does.
There are intense Nutraceuticals
that we use such as Flavon from
Hungary and of course the
Kangen water alkaline by
ionization providing lots of
molecular hydrogen giving the
water powerful antioxidant
properties. All these products
are obtained on the Internet and
are marketed through
relationship marketing. We tell
people about the products and
they buy the products and they
tell people about the products.
We have been excellent
consumers but our network
marketing skills remain to be

seen. About six months after my mom passed we were out of the money that she left us and I couldn't make the mortgage payments. We went in and out of foreclosure status for the next eight years! The housing market collapsed in 2008 and we were right in the middle of it. I attempted multiple times to obtain a loan modification but we were running around in circles only able to delay foreclosure. I couldn't describe what we went through but I followed the directions of a close friend of ours whom we met at Agape. She was learning about real estate investing and could delay foreclosures on her properties. I'm good at acting and following directions so

when she told me to file
something with the court I filed
it!

MST

It wasn't until 2012 that we
had mandatory classes on
Military Sexual Trauma (MST).
At that point I hadn't even
identified what happened to me
as a gang rape or even thinking
of it as connected with military
service. I was simply crazy...had
Bipolar Disorder and
periodically became unraveled
when under stress. One of the
definitions of MST was that you
were serving in the military at
the time of your rape. You didn't
necessarily have to be raped by

military people! The thought started to form in my head as I had flashbacks. I was raped...I wasn't sure who I could tell. I brought it up to my therapist and he pointed out that it was a long time ago. The two of us worked so hard stabilizing me that he was concerned that if I started talking about it that I might un-stabilize. I brought it up to one of my co-workers. "Girl! You are sitting on a gold mine!!!" He meant I should go apply for compensation. I wasn't thinking of that. I was trying to push the flashbacks and memories out of my head. I don't want to talk about this to people. I was feeling ashamed. It took about a year for me to start dealing with it and only because

I was unraveling again. I fell at work. I slipped on Surgilube Lubricant. Someone had carelessly and neglectfully left two open packets of the lubricant on the floor by the door of the emergency room at the VA. I went downstairs from the psychiatric unit to check a patient's belongings for contraband and sharps as they were being admitted to the psychiatric unit. I walked through the door of the emergency room and my foot hit the open packets of lubricant and I did a banana peel number with my feet in the air and my lower back hitting the floor. I tucked my head but when I hit the floor my head jerked back in whiplash fashion. It must have looked hilarious. The people behind the desk watched me and laughed. The security guard came over and said, "Oh oh...you filing for Worker's Comp. now!" I was full of adrenaline and didn't think much about it. I had work to get done. I felt bruised but could move. I went back to work but filled out the paperwork for injury as I was asked to do when I reported the fall to my supervisor.

The next morning I woke up feeling like I had been hit by a truck. I couldn't move my neck!!! I went to work and was sent to Employee Health. I waited several hours to be seen...in an **empty** waiting room! No X-rays were ordered. They told me to take some

Motrin and go back to work. I went to a chiropractor and got my neck to move again, but something was very wrong. I just thought I was bruised. I went back to work thinking I would get better. Everyday my lower back felt like I had been kicked by a horse. I started to have headaches again. The pain didn't get better...it got worse! I left work crying because the pain became so intense. I couldn't work. The bending to get medications out of the medication cart or to help a patient with making their bed aggravated the pain. My life was changed. I would never be the same.

I was out on Worker's Compensation for 8 months. I

wasn't paid anything until about 4 months. During that time, I lost my Nissan Altima, as I was unable to make payments on it. When I finally received the back payments, I was able to get a second-hand Ford Escape Hybrid. My emotions became unstable again dealing with pain day in and day out. I hadn't been on any medication for about a year as I was doing well. Since Darwin had moved in I was getting healthier. The turning point for me happened when I was seeing a doctor at Brotman who suggested to lose weight I have my stomach cut up into a Fobi pouch! What part of this was healthy?! I would be at risk for infections and have nutrition deficits. At that point when I still had my mom with me I began to consider "Alternative Medicine." I think natural things should be the primary mode of healing and only when those holistic practices don't work does one try petroleum-based pharmaceuticals. I started with Herbalife and Big Planet but soon found the LifeWave patches. I knew Darwin would appreciate them. He was busy with school at the time and didn't look at the information. After he graduated and moved in he became the patch expert and was one of the few people in the company who could use the principles of Asian Medicine and acupuncture to help people with their specific conditions. Between the Nutraceuticals and patches I could wean off medication. Being injured and in pain was a whole other story. I refused pain medication because I didn't want narcotics around to ruminate about overdosing on them should I have a period of despair. I used pain patches effectively and major antioxidants like Kangen water and Turmeric (Ukon sold by Enagic the Kangen water company). I even used essential oils such as eucalyptus and black pepper for the pain. However, the chronic pain made me edgy. The Worker's Comp doctor was pushing me to go back to work and I wanted to tell him first I needed to be back on some psychiatric medication to be able to deal effectively with the pain and stress of the VA politics. I started to speak to him and he literally held up his hand "speak to the hand" and walked out of the room. I was so distraught I started to cry and wandered out of the room into the staff kitchen. I leaned over the sink and saw a dull cake knife. I picked it up and tried to jab it into my arm. One of the other doctors saw this and called for help. Soon after the swat team arrived. They carted me off to UCLA emergency room where Darwin eventually picked me up. The 10 minutes the doctor in a big hurry saved was wasted in the 45 minutes he had his office close down with all the drama. I soon restarted taking antidepressants and a mood stabilizer and returned to work at the VA on light duty.

Somehow this doctor reported what happened in his office to the VA Human Resources and I was questioned about it. I think this is a violation of HIPPA laws. What happened because of an illness in the doctor's office needs to be kept confidential. I hadn't threatened anyone at work where the need for a Tarasoff report was necessary! As I was talking to the director I mentioned that I suffered from flashbacks and nightmares from military sexual trauma and she referred me to the MST support group. I had had no idea there was a support group at the VA for that. It took me another two weeks to track it down and find out where it met. Then I began to go to the MST support group regularly while I was on light duty.

Strength

MST group is an amazing group of women who are survivors. We all have pain of our rapes in common but each of us copes with it in our own unique ways. There are common threads and understandable beliefs we have developed over time. It surprised me that I wasn't the only one who didn't talk to anyone about their rape for 30 years!!! There were more women around my age in this group than there were younger women. It was not unusual to repress the trauma for years and years!

I was not the only one labeled "crazy" or miss-diagnosed. It was common practice to put "Character Disorder" on the DD214 military discharge papers! I was not alone with this dark secret and I started to talk about the gang rape, the date rapes and the rape on the boat. At first I was very emotional. I mentioned my swimsuit torn to shreds on the floor in a corner of my apartment after the gang rape and I was hysterical sobbing and releasing the intense emotion I was feeling. We have a rule in group not to hand the Kleenex box to someone as that may shut down their crying and they need to release. I thought the pain would never end. One of the women offered to help me work on getting compensation for MST. I was asked to write about what happened to me! At this point I wasn't even able to say the word rape. I referred to it as the traumatic event. I was the first in the group to use the words Gang Rape. Another woman thanked me. Although she had never thought about saying she was Gang raped she also had 3 attackers who raped her. Calling it a Gang Rape was helpful to her to wrap her mind around what had happened to her. She talked about a scar she still had on her body from being beaten up. I took my shoe off and showed the therapist the scar from a cigarette burn on my foot from the Gang Rape. I have always tried to hid it and not wear certain types of sandals. I listened to other women talk about their rapes every Monday. I was amazed some of them had relationships with men, marriages and children. Some had children from the rape. Some of the women had been raped multiple different times like me. Like myself quite a few felt they will never have a relationship with a man or get married. I gained strength from these women. They are my sisters. We are soldier girls who each fought our own individual battles for survival and won. I write this book to reach out to other women. For those who have not yet articulated to anyone what they have been through, you are not alone. For the men and women out there who don't understand rape? I'm glad to share with you. It's through the education and talking about rape that we will raise consciousness and awareness so that the culture of rape whether it is in the military or at universities will diminish. Rape is a very heinous and destructive act. It deeply damages the victim and changes their life forever. As a survivor, I've learned from the group that there is a new "normal" for those who have been raped. We have been changed but with help and support of others we can overcome the challenges before us.

Educating Others

I started teaching nursing students part time after a few years working at the VA and continue to do this part time. The young fresh enthusiasm for nursing that they have keeps me going. I feel privileged to have the opportunity to be an influence on the future of nursing by educating new nurses. I recently had one of my students tell me she was interested in working with rape survivors when she graduated. I told her about my being gang raped in the Air Force and shared that when I went for help

I was labeled "crazy woman" and kicked out. I encouraged her by saying good help for rape trauma survivors is very much needed and I was happy to hear that she wanted to build a career in that direction. It gives me hope that things have changed. MST survivors can now come to the VA and receive help. I wished I didn't have to wait 30 years, but it's good. I'm glad things are moving in the right direction for the next generation. I would like to be a part of this progressive movement and writing this book has been a part of this. It took some guts to write it all down. After having gone through Cognitive-Behavioral Processing Therapy (CPT), I have been able to piece together the puzzle of my life and have more clarity. CPT for MST was difficult and very painful. We had to write details about our rape and read it over and over to ourselves. My friend who helped me hold onto my house for years gave me the support to read it out loud. She is used to the structure of Alcoholics Anonymous (AA) and used it to help me with a process that was very much like the 4th step. During the process, I experienced intense emotion and could identify triggers that set me off. As the denial of what happened to me became less the depression increased. I was having intense suicidal ideation again and brought myself to the ER. I was off work for 2 months.

I needed to go back to work for loss of income and the psychiatrist suggested that I work a 4-day workweek. I was better but not quite stable. When Human Resources (HR) denied ever getting the letter from the psychiatrist and told me that when I ran out of sick time and leave time I was considered AWOL I flashed back to the military where I went in for help and was not understood. I imploded and had a meltdown recently and was so upset that I didn't think through my saying I was going to overdose on the narcotics at the domiciliary or the "DOM" where I had been successfully working after coming off light duty. I realized I was unstable and went to see the psychiatrist. She had me do some deep breathing to calm me down and then sent me back to work. On the way to work my supervisor called me and wanted to know where I was. The police picked me up and took me to the ER where another psychiatrist cleared me to go back to work. My therapist said to me, "Heidi, you want to kill the feelings...not yourself." I would agree with that for the most part when I'm feeling that intensely I want the feeling to end. I started to take a class for people "who lose it in HR." It has been helpful and I realize when I'm that upset I shouldn't push myself to get things done. I can always do whatever it was I needed to do the next day when

I'm calmer. I went to work the next day and I was pulled off work. Just like I was in the Air Force where I was put in the library to type up cards! I now am sitting at a desk at the Transfer Center putting in Non-VA Care Hospital Notification Notes whenever the fax from another non-VA facility comes in. I'm supposed to be evaluated in a few more days by a doctor to see if I can go back to work at the DOM again. Later this week I take my nursing students to Mental Health Court for their mental health legal experience.

The DOM

I started working at the DOM about a year and a half ago after coming off light duty, following my back and neck injuries from slipping on Surgilube negligently left on the ER floor. One thing I found challenging was working on my boundary issues. There was an elderly man named Mr. Wildon whose first words to me the first day I worked there were, "Welcome to Hell." I said, "No...Hell is where I was. This is purgatory!" We bonded. There was transference going on as he just lost his daughter who was a nurse my age. He talked to me about the death of his wife from cancer and his fear of dying. I started doing small favors for him. "Can you give me some tape? I need a battery. While you're picking up the battery can you get some soda?" Before I knew it, to have good rapport, I was running out during my shift to get him a McDonald's Hamburger! How did this happen? One thing I learned in group is that when you're raped your boundaries are violated and somehow this affects your sense of self and what is appropriate and what is not appropriate. Also, there is a connection between rape and body image and being overweight as a sort of protection. I can't quite grasp that one yet as I am still overweight and although I eat healthy I eat a lot. Maybe someday I'll be able to let go of the excess weight. I took a big step stopping the running errands for Mr. Wildon. He told me he needed soda and the sidewalks to the store were too uneven for him on which to ride his cart. I validated him and said, "Yes the sidewalks are uneven." But I didn't run to offer picking up soda for him on my way to work. I felt bad for him but it was a big step for me in establishing boundaries. I also stopped accepting gifts from him as well. That was real difficult. I didn't want to hurt his feelings. I don't know if I'll be able to go back to the DOM. I'd like to. I don't move around enough in a desk job and my schedule might change to a day shift during the weekdays. That would affect my teaching during the week, where I need to have weekdays off to do this. At the DOM, I'm getting up and down all the time getting medications, doing dressing changes, triaging patients and giving first aid. I burn off more calories. The next chapter will be written after the evaluation from the doctor, so we will see what happens!

Post Evaluation

Evaluation went well. I brought my latest Proficiency Report with me in which I had received a High Satisfactory on interpersonal relationships. This is very rare at the VA. You could part the Red Sea and management still will give the employee a **Satisfactory**. Linear with no deviation **Sat-is-factory...** To me this means of course you sit on your butt and don't do very much. I can't be that way. I tend to get involved with compassion. I finally had a supervisor who recognized my efforts! The doctor at Occupational Health seemed to understand; however, he wants a letter from my psychiatrist stating that I can return to my workstation at the DOM or I can't return to my workstation at the DOM. In the mean time, I will be learning some new skills at the transfer center having this desk job. If I

have the paycheck coming in
Darwin and I will be all right. My
compensation for Military
Sexual Trauma-Post Traumatic
Stress Disorder almost covers
the exorbitant mortgage
payments. If it wasn't for the
compensation, we wouldn't have
been able to obtain a workable
loan modification. It took me
almost 3 years submitting my
claim and resubmitting my claim
to finally become service
connected and able to receive
treatment and medical care at
the VA! Service connection
means the injury for which you
receive treatment and medical
care is connected to your service
in the military. I went from
being a "non-veteran" who was
only in the service 18 months to

being a disabled veteran with medical benefits. I am grateful for the help I received at the VA. I could not have written this book without it. I just wish it were available 30 years earlier. I might have not had so many years of suffering and feeling as if I was "crazy woman." I still want to get my DD214 changed as I wasn't discharged for a **"Character Disorder"** or **"Substandard Performance of Duty"** as all my evaluations in the Air Force was **Standard** or **Above Standard**. I don't know why but I have a need to set the record straight! Thanks to my MST group I know I'm not alone. I know a few of them were also labeled with a "Character Disorder" and discharged from the Military after they were raped. I have hope that my experience will help someone out there. You are not alone. Talk to someone. Tell other people what happened. We need to be heard. Rape needs to be an uncommon trauma not a common one. 1 in 100 men (1%) in the military are raped and 1 in 4 women (25%) in the military are raped! The more that people know that this happens frequently the easier it will be for people to receive help. Programs can be instituted to raise consciousness and prevent rape's happening. When perpetrators get away with it they are likely to do it again and other rapists feel protected as well when there is a culture of rape in the environment. One of the triggers for my writing this book was a comment from one of my patients, a male veteran that stated in surprise, "Rape doesn't happen in the military!" There is a need for people in the military to be educated about military sexual trauma (MST). The increased awareness can prevent cohorts from abusing women and some men, as more people will understand the consequences that rape has in affecting other's lives. If we keep silent and don't bring it out in the open the longer the violence will continue.

Epilogue
(They Haven't Changed
in 30 Years)

They fired me for my disability....! I'm writing this over a year later. It feels like a repeat of the military. I'm still trying to wrap my head around what happened. When I previously wrote I was aware that my psychiatrist was supposed to write something for me to be able to go back to the DOM and work again as a nurse. The only letter that I remember was my VA psychiatrist Dr. Yeager had written a letter for me to have a four-day workweek to decrease some of the stress. I don't remember the employee health doctor giving me a letter to give to my therapists to have them write something. I continued to work at the transfer center from April 2017- August 2017. By August I felt I had stabilized and I wrote an e-mail to the Director of Mental health after my coworker called me and complained that they were very short staffed and they all wanted me back. One of the stress factors I experienced before I left was working by myself in the nurse's station for months while my coworker was traveling to Nigeria. Another stress factor was excessive bending obtaining medication out of the lower drawers of the Omni-cell. The repetitive bending was exacerbating the injury I originally had from the fall when I slipped on Surgilube lubricant left on the floor of the ER. I learned that since I left they had now moved the medications up to the drawers, which were at least waist level. My coworker was back from Nigeria, the drawers of medication were higher so I would not have to bend excessively, and I had stabilized from Cognitive Processing Therapy (CPT). So I was ready to go back.

I explained this in the e-mail to the Director of Mental Health. The next day I was sent back to the DOM but not in patient care! The Nurse Manager informed me that I would have to have a "Fit For Duty Test" before going back to patient care. So from August 2017-October 2017 I assisted the Nurse Manager updating admission lists, developing an orientation check list and various power points for nursing educational purposes. The Nurse Manager wasn't clear on what was going on. She couldn't answer my questions and even the employee health doctor couldn't explain to me why my own therapists couldn't just write a note that I could go back to work in patient care. Nobody at that time asked me for a letter from my doctors. The employee health doctor said, "We tried that before." I didn't understand what he was talking about. What did we try before? I had no memory of his asking me to provide a letter from my doctors that he apparently had done back in April 2017 when I was still undergoing CPT treatment! In August when I asked why I couldn't just provide a letter from my doctors I was met with vague statements, no clarification and avoidance! I continued to be isolated from my coworkers and told not to go into patient care areas. I was to stay in the conference room down the hallway from the nurse's station. Then I came into work October 4th 2017 and told the next day I would be doing my "Fitness For Duty Test" in Encino. The employee health doctor had explained that as he was not competent in the area of psychiatric testing he could not evaluate me properly so I was impelled to drive to Encino to be evaluated by a psychologist who did testing to vet cadets to the LAPD police academy!

Psychiatric Testing Again!

I arrived at the testing office on October 5, 2017 at 8 am in Encino. I requested to speak first to the evaluating psychologist as this whole experience was bringing me back to the psychiatric testing that was done to me in the

military. The situation was a
trigger for my PTSD. The people
in the office told me "that is not
the way it is done." I was to
complete 7 different
psychological tests before seeing
the evaluating psychologist. The
other people in the office were
dressed in business attire and
looking very professional. I was
Heidiesque casual which meant
bright colors and comfortable. I
was in the wrong place. These
people were going for jobs as
police officers! They brought me
to a room with a large window
and a conference room table and
chairs. I was given a stack of
tests and 2 pencils. I couldn't
focus. This was awful. I was
back in the military trying to
prove my sanity and not be

kicked out. I was crying through a good part of the testing. I couldn't think clearly. I felt so overwhelmed I had to leave the room and went down the hallway. There was a balcony. I looked over the railing. I thought about jumping off the balcony to my death. Knowing me I'd probably survive and be a paraplegic. I called my brother Darwin. He was very grounding and calm. He suggested I take a break for lunch. I went back and informed the office drones that I was going to take a break for lunch. Could they not see how upset I was? Earlier that morning a woman had walked into the room when I was standing at the window crying and stated she was looking for someone named Robert. Later to find out that this was the psychologist. She didn't introduce herself. I would have liked to speak to her and not be treated so indifferently. I walked to Gelson's down the street and filled my plate with comfort food...macaroni and cheese.

Toward the end of the testing around 3 pm while I was working on The Minnesota Multiphasic Personality Inventory-2 (MMPI), the evaluating psychologist came into the room and told me I could finish later and that she wanted to evaluate me. I explained to her that this situation was stressful as it was a reminder of the testing I went through in the Air Force. This situation was a trigger for my PTSD. She seemed to understand. She said I didn't have to finish the testing. The MMPI is an extremely tedious test asking repeated questions. Do you love your father? Do you hate your mother? Do you like the color orange? Are you kind to cats? Do you think your feet are too big? I much prefer the fill in the blank tests where I can create my own answer. I was relieved to get out of there and go home.

Several days later the employee health doctor notified me to come see him. He sat behind the safety of his desk and disclosed to me the results of the testing: "UNFIT FOR DUTY." I was appalled. How could she find me unfit for duty? Didn't the psychologist understand that the testing was done under duress? My own doctors and psychologists were all in favor of my going back to patient care. The difference is that they knew me! This evaluating psychologist was basing the evaluation on how I was under duress! She didn't get that I've been working as a psychiatric nurse for 30 years?! I was unfit for duty as a police officer but not as a psychiatric nurse! The employee health doctor saw my reaction and asked in a very condescending tone, "Oh...do you need to go to the ER now?" I told him that remark was very condescending. He came up with the bullshit that he was trying to provide appropriate care. Just ridiculous! How about appropriately responding to my feelings of shock and horror! It was happening to me again! I was being labeled "crazy woman" and the next thing was that they were going to boot me out!

I received an offer of reassignment for a program coordinator. This would have been fine except that the pay was $30,000 a year less then I was making now!!! So you're demoting me to a non-nursing position!!! I have my nursing license! I refused and started looking for another nursing job. The VA kept me in the conference room like I had leprosy or something. I was not to go anywhere near patient care areas. Many times the staff would come to the conference room seeking my advice or input on a patient care issue. Unfit for Duty...Really? I developed a Detox training program for both staff and nurses to establish the protocol for dealing with the "New Detox Program" being established. At least 15 new nurses were hired. There were now 2-3 nurses doing the job that I had done by myself. By January I thought I would be out of there and I started a new job as a Nurse Manager at a rehabilitation center north of Korea Town. When I arrived they expected me to part the red sea and walk on water at the same time. The first day I had minimal orientation on how to get onto their system. I figured out enough to receive orders from a doctor and enter it into the system. I repeated the orders back to the doctor and documented what he told me. Between the beeping call lights and uncertainty of what I was supposed to do I went home crying. It was very stressful. I returned the next day to be told by the Director of nursing that they did not have time to orient me! The Director of nursing said that the doctor claimed that the labs he ordered last night were to be STAT! At no time did he say STAT to me. I told her this and her response was, "Well that's not what he said!" So the doctor threw me under the bus!

They rescinded my contract and I went back to the VA after my vacation and leave time was all used up. I continued the next two months presenting educational material to staff and nurses. I did a presentation on therapeutic communication skills and customer service and I presented the material for the detox program as well. I was asked by the Nurse Manager to supervise or be a "resource person" to the staff on day shift on the weekends as the supervisor that had been there left. I made rounds and checked in with staff and nursing to make sure everything was covered. At one point a tall man with hyperactive melanocytes (my way of indicating this man had a dark complexion) was very hostile toward me. "You act like we don't know how to do our job!" Believe me that was not my intent. I'm just trying to find a place for myself. So I'm unfit for duty yet a supervising resource person...nothing makes sense here.

I was confronted one day by the robots that managed the DOM to sign over my medical records from the Encino evaluation to the Physical Standards Board at the VA. They were just "following orders" of course. They both gave me a blank stare and said, "We are trying to help you." Help me!!! Really? I refused to sign. I was then scheduled an appointment with the Director of the VA

Medical Center. After I had not received a response from the Director of Mental Health I had gone up to the administration offices up on the 6th floor where they hide behind bulletproof glass and requested a meeting with the Director of the VA West Los Angeles Medical Center. I did this long before I was sent on the psychological evaluation. I never received a response from her either after being told she would contact me. Now after the testing and being labeled unfit for duty she wanted to meet with me! The only purpose of that meeting was to coerce me into signing over the records from the Encino evaluation. I was told that I would be fired that day if I did not sign over the records. I could not get a copy of these records or find out what the specific results were. I tried with the less than helpful union to which I had been paying dues and who did nothing to help me! During the meeting with the Director of the VA West Los Angeles Medical Center I was told directly to my face by the Director that, "Promotion is not an option for you." I had been applying for management and nurse educator positions unsuccessfully at the VA. I have a Master's Degree in Nursing Administration and Education. Why is a position as a Nurse Manager or a Nurse Educator not an option for me? I hadn't done anything wrong. I went for help. I had a bad moment in HR.

I was never a threat to patients. All my evaluations are standard or above. I have done nothing but a good job being a nurse here for the last 12 years. Now with my back injury and having gone through treatment for PTSD I'm unfit for duty!

Hi Mr. Doelling,

This is message is my response to the "Fitness for Duty" recommendation of Dr. Meredith Rimmer after her psychological evaluation, dated October 10, 2017. To say I am "unfit for duty" as a staff nurse is extremely **vague and inaccurate**. During Cognitive Processing Therapy (CPT) with Dr. Himmelfarb four months ago, for Military Sexual Trauma (MST), suicidal ideation surfaced. Passing out narcotics and having suicidal ideation was not a good idea. I believe removing me from patient care was a good thing to do **at that time**. The combination of depression from MST triggered by going through CPT and recalling the details of being gang rapped in the Air Force plus the physical pain from excessive bending at work which exacerbated my back injury from the fall November 4th, 2014 where I had slipped on 2 open packets of Surgilube lubricant someone had negligently left on the floor of the ER at the West Los Angeles VA while I was working and incurred injury to both my neck and back was **extremely stressful**. After the rapes in the Air Force I went for help. The Air Force reaction to my asking for help was to have me undergo psychiatric testing after psychiatric testing. I was labeled "crazy" and honorably discharged from the Air Force, because MST was not recognized 30 years ago, by the Air Force. The psychological testing done in Encino recently reminded of that time in the Air Force. However, I certainly understand your concern about my being safe around narcotics. The fact is I have been a psychiatric nurse for over 30 years. I have always been a very responsible and prudent nurse. I have never jeopardized patient care. I have been competent and there has never been a complaint about my judgement or behavior. I will always ask for help if I feel overwhelmed and unable to cope, which is why I checked into the ER as the suicidal ideation surfaced during my CPT with Dr. Himmelfarb. My strength is in interpersonal relationships and teaching. I have been teaching UCLA nursing students from 2007-2015 and Mount Saint Mary's Nursing Students from 2015- the present in their psychiatric clinical rotations. I understand your concern for liability in my going back to passing out medication although, I feel very capable now in doing so. I believe I would be best utilized in teaching and education. I have repeatedly applied for nursing educator positions and management positions here at the West Los Angeles VA attempting to minimize my exposure to passing out medications and focusing on my interpersonal relationship and teaching strengths. I also have an interest in Natural Medicine which is congruent with the direction that the VA wants to go. Please, let's have a win-win situation here where I can be utilized in education or management, or both. I know I will be a successful leader and educator for the Veteran's Administration, as I have already been working at the VA for eleven years.

If you want a more accurate psychological recommendation you may talk to Dr. Himmelfarb whom I have been working with here at the West Los Angeles VA for MST issues for over two years and my therapist for over 15 years, Dr. Stephan Poulter (310) 480-8352. They both know me quite well and know what my capabilities are and I'm sure that they would agree with the point of view which I have articulated here, namely that I am quite psychologically fit to be a staff nurse at the VA and would function optimally as a nurse educator and/or nurse manager.

Thank you,
Heidi Lobstein MSN, RN
(310) 902-4555

Honorable Discharge

The Physical Standards Board found me Unfit For Duty despite my turning in letters from 3 psychologists, 2 psychiatrists, 1 Nurse Manager and a Coworker all saying that I did an excellent job as a nurse and that I had been going through treatment for MST/PTSD and as expected had been emotionally labile but since then had stabilized and could go back to patient care. The Physical Standards Board based their decision on a psychologist who spoke to me for 20 minutes while I was under duress from a battery of 7 different psychological exams.

According to my brother Darwin, who earned a PhD at Purdue University using psychometric tests such as the MMPI, told me that these tests are not always testing accurately and have to be taken into context of the situation. I was separated for my disability April 20, 2018. I thought this was not legal to do! I consulted with a lawyer who told me that because I am a healthcare professional I am under a different set of laws! I was informed that the EEOC case I filed would take 2 years for them to complete the investigation! A lawyer will not take the case until the EEOC case has been investigated. In the mean time I tried Hospice

Nursing. I like the part of being present and supportive as a person is transitioning. It was the bending to do the patient care, the long hours driving around from patient to patient that lived far from each other and very little pay. I couldn't do it. I will be teaching in the fall. I have 3 clinical courses to teach in Psychiatric Nursing rather than just the one clinical as I did when I worked at the VA. I applied for Medical Retirement from the VA. I was told that this takes 6 months to a year to kick in. I have the compensation to live off but we are falling behind on the mortgage. I have a social worker at the VA who has connected me with possible resources. My main concern is the house. I'm working with the bank on reworking another loan modification.

I've been trying to get the "Character Disorder" and "Substandard Performance of Duty" changed on my DD214 discharge papers from the Air Force. It's not enough for me to have an Honorable Discharged. I was coerced by the JAG Lawyer in the military to sign papers, if I didn't I wouldn't have an Honorable Discharge. I was coerced to sign over confidential medical records from the Encino psychological exam to the Physical Standards Board under the threat of being fired. I was fired anyway. I feel in both cases I was treated unjustly. I recently received a response from the military that they continue to deny changing anything on my DD214 claiming I was fraudulent about a preexisting mental condition based on the records that I had given the counselor in the military thinking she would help me clarify things. It is truly an insane world we live in where one who seeks help to better oneself and grow is considered "crazy" yet the people who adapt to a reactive impersonal bureaucracy (bureau-crazy) are normal! I will continue to move forward in my life and grow. I think it is important that I help pave the way for future people and future nurses seeking help for military sexual trauma so that others don't get steamrolled

over by the system. It is time for
cultural change:
#me too/military sexual trauma

Made in the USA
San Bernardino, CA
19 January 2019